Written by Alexandra Colley

and the pupils of the Stamford Endowed Schools
(past and present)

Dedicated to Canon John Duncan Day

Headmaster 1913 – 1947

In grateful and loving memory of those
staff and boys who gave their lives

Christ Me Spede

In November 2014 each pupil of Stamford School
received a copy of this book as a gift from the Stamford School
Re-Endowment Fund.

First published 2014

The Stamford Endowed Schools
Brazenose House
St Paul's Street
Stamford
Lincolnshire
PE9 2BS

www.ses.lincs.sch.uk

ISBN 978-0-9930581-0-3

Design by Design Partners Creative Ltd

Contents

Foreword

Mr W M Phelan, Headmaster of Stamford School

It is a great honour for me to write the foreword for this book. As an historian, I have sto
on the battlefields of the First World War on countless occasions, with countless schoolbo;
but the scale of the human tragedy that was the First World War can make it difficult i
us today to gain a clear impression of the experiences and characters of the individua
who fought and died in it. The individual portraits in this book, however, give us a valuak
insight into the personalities of the Old Stamfordians to whose memory this publication
dedicated.

The qualities which we hold dear in Stamfordians today can be found in the obituaries
those who were lost. As an example, Thomas Francis Senescall, a Private in the Suffc
regiment, who was killed in action in France in August 1917, was noted as being:

"universally and deservedly popular. Without attaining a position of speci
prominence he was a genuine trier, gifted with a particularly bright and geni
disposition and could always be relied on to do his best "

I could give any number of current Stamfordians who would fit this description today.

It beholds me to speak a little about the colossus of Stamford School, Canon John Dunc;
Day, also known as "The Gaffer." I feel some affinity with him as, he taught, like me,
Warwick School before he came to Stamford. I spent every Sunday in the same Chapel
which he was Chaplain for six years. At Warwick School we had a "black book" giving tl
details and stories of all who had fallen in the two wars, and it is right that our story, tl
Stamfordian story, is now brought together and told in the same way in these pages.

In the valete in the Stamfordian it was said of Canon Day that he:

"had a genius for improvisation in the face of unforeseeable difficulties"

and this would have helped him stay the course through the loss and melancholy
the two world wars which it was his lot to endure. It is obvious when reading Canc
Day's words in the Stamfordian on the Fallen that it did affect him greatly. It notes th
the deaths of boys were always announced by Day in assembly:

"We used to have assembly in the mornings in the chapel and you could always te
when one of the lads had been killed by the way he walked in and the way he walke
up to the lectern. Often, the fallen boy would have left the School the previous year an
on such an occasion, the hymn was always "O God our help in ages past.""

This hymn was used because of the poignancy of the verse which is reproduced on the bac
of this book.

It is a testament to the man that he saw the school through both world wars with th
associated loss of staff and boys. I would have found this an impossible task.

hope that you will find something in this book which will resonate with you. It is a
ompendium of the short lives of those brave Stamfordians who were lost. But for me, it is
eir connections with the school, the teams they were in, the comments made about them,
here they lived, which road, which house, which helped me to link with them.

s is clear here, many of the casualties in the Great War were not professional soldiers –
eir 100,000 numbers had been exhausted by 1915 – but the conscripted army of Lord
tchener, he of the *"Your country needs you"* posters. The Germans called the first battle
Ypres *"Kindermort Zu Ypren"* translated as *"The slaughter of the innocents"* I cannot
ink of a more apt way to describe those lost and injured in World War One.

ill Phelan
outhfields House
amford School

pril 2014

he memorial plaque in St. George's memorial Church, Ypres, dedicated to the memory of
e Old Stamfordians who laid down their lives in the First World War.

Introduction

On August 4th 1914, a war was declared that would forever change the world in which ⟨we⟩ live. Over 50 Stamfordians – both staff members and school boys – would die in, or a⟨s a⟩ result of, the years of fighting that followed.

This book tries to bring those men back to life. It is important to remember them as mu⟨ch⟩ more than just a name on a war memorial or in a passage from the Stamfordian magazine⟨. It⟩ is important to think of the many lives that they touched and the impact that their lives a⟨nd⟩ their deaths had on the town and on the school community.

The Stamfordian magazine covers the war years with a strong sense of patriotism and giv⟨es⟩ accounts of rousing talks and speeches and long lists of boys who went off to serve th⟨eir⟩ country. However, the magazines also give deeply moving accounts of the lives that were l⟨ost⟩ and many of the obituaries, most of them written by the Headmaster Canon Day, are still ⟨as⟩ personal and poignant as when they were first written. These accounts have provided mu⟨ch⟩ of the information included here and give an invaluable insight into life at the school dur⟨ing⟩ the changing and perilous years of the war.

Of course, history is not without its flaws, and some of those who sacrificed their lives s⟨till⟩ remain relatively unknown to us. I have tried to include information on their address⟨es⟩ and their families from the census records, and I have included any reference to them in t⟨he⟩ Stamfordian magazines that exist.

Many local and national websites have conducted their own research and have helped ⟨to⟩ signpost other records that have provided useful information, and I am grateful to all tho⟨se⟩ who have been so willing to help and offer advice.

Any omissions or mistakes are most definitely not intentional – my hope is that t⟨his⟩ provides a link to the past and sets future generations on the road to researching the⟨se⟩ names and adding to the information included here. It is by no means a comprehensi⟨ve⟩ account and I am sure that, as further records become available, the information will ⟨be⟩ continually revised. I hope it is, at least, an accessible tribute to those men who walked t⟨he⟩ halls of the school over 100 years ago.

It has been a privilege to spend time among the Stamfordians listed here. They ha⟨ve⟩ provided humour, sporting and academic prowess, bravery and unstinting coura⟨ge.⟩ Their sacrifice is deeply humbling.

As Canon Day said to the boys of the school at a memorial service in November 1915:

"their lives must and ought to have an influence on (our) own and ... (we) should stri⟨ve⟩ in (our) own feeble way to reproduce the best of their characters... (Their) lives m⟨ust⟩ leave a permanent and abiding mark on the history of the school"

I sincerely hope that this is the case.

Alexandra Colley
April 2014

cknowledgements

is book would not have been possible without the help of a number of people who have
ded, indicated and offered support during the research process and beyond.

stly, the initial research of Nick McCarthy (OS), who finalised the correct roll of honour
d who also provided many of the photos included in this book, was extremely helpful,
d I thank him very much for this.

must also acknowledge the ongoing support of the Stamford School History
partment – especially Mr Dan Stamp and the vital early research of the pupils – Eleanor
ompson, Sam Gostick, Charles Bennie and Jonathan Evans. Also, the Stamford Endowed
hools' Foundation – especially Rachael Petrie and Adam Cox (OS) for their guidance,
vice and support and the provision of original materials, design resource and artwork.

so Rev. Mark Goodman, the School Chaplain, Alister Pike, Geoffrey Brown and the
admaster, Will Phelan for their ideas, help and encouragement. Thank you also to the
arders of Byard House (2013 – 14) for their constant questions and inquisitiveness about
photos and research covering my desk and the many boys who have been on battlefields
ps over the years and provided better insights than we could ever imagine.

yond the school, I must thank Agata Czaczka and Gillian Fewings of St Mark and St John
llege archives in Plymouth. I am also grateful to Sheila Bartas, relative of Arthur Claydon,
the information and pictures provided. The contribution of Rory Langan (OS) is obvious
the information included on the Lincolnshire Regiment and the Hohenzollern Redoubt,
d I thank him for his commitment and enthusiasm. I must also acknowledge the brilliant
search of Michael Walsh, author of *Brothers in War*, a fantastic book on the Beechey
others, which helped to reinforce our own records and link to others that we may have
ssed!

a personal note, thank you to Donnie Taggart for his information on World War One
edals and the CWGC, Mrs Fiona Spong and Mr David Lennie for proofreading the final
aft, and, finally, thank you to my husband, David Colley, for putting up with my Sunday
ght research sessions and accompanying me around more graveyards and churches than
an count!

lexandra Colley
oril 2014

Timeline 1914 – 1924

Those in **bold** are the names of the Fallen.

1914

June	28th	Assassination of Archduke Franz Ferdinand
August	3rd	Germany declares war on France
	4th	Britain declares war on Germany
	7th	Kitchener calls for 100,000 men to join the army
	22nd	BEF lands in France
	23rd	Battle of Mons
	c. 24th	**Victor-André Grivel**
September	6th	First Battle of Marne
	25th	Battle of Albert
	31st	German troops invade Amiens
October	1st	Battle of Arras
	15th	First Battle of Ypres (lasts until November 11th)
November	22nd	Trenches established along the entire Western Front
December	16th	German fleet attacks Hartlepool, Whitby and Scarborough

1915

January	19th	First air attacks on Britain – Zeppelins bomb Great Yarmouth and King's Lynn
February	19th	Naval bombardment begins in Gallipoli
March	10th	Battle of Neuve Chapelle
	18th	Allied attack on the Dardanelles
April	22nd	Second Battle of Ypres (lasts until May 25th)
	25th	Allied forces land at Gallipoli
May	9th	Artois Offensive
June	22nd	**George Griffiths**
	30th	Germans use flame throwers against the British trenches at Hooge

August	6th	Offensive at Suvla Bay, Gallipoli
	21st	Battle of Scimater Hill, Gallipoli
	21st	**Horace Curtis** (wounded)
September	25th	Battle of Loos (lasts until October 8th)
	25th	**Barnard Beechey**
	26th	**Leonard Pitt**
	27th	British and Canadian troops take Hill 70 at Loos
October	13th	Attack to capture Hohenzollern Redoubt begins
	13th – 16th	**Charles Gray, Arthur Evans, Charles Bird, Charles Knight**
November	3rd	**Harold Springthorpe**

1916

January	24th	Introduction of Conscription Act (becomes law 25th May)
February	21st	The Battle of Verdun (lasts until 16th December)
April		Fighting around Mount St Eloi
	21st	**William Wright**
May	31st	Battle of Jutland (lasts until June 1st)
June	4th	**Francis Whincup; Geoffrey Jones**
July	1st	The Battle of the Somme (lasts until November 18th)
	5th	Fighting in Mametz Wood
	8th	**Arthur Cowie**
	19th	**Albert Blades**
	23rd	Battle of Pozières (lasts until August 7th)
August	4th	**Albert Curtis**
September	8th	**Aubrey Glew**
	25th – 28th	Battle of Morval
	26th	**Charles Lowe**

October	18th	Battle of Le Transloy
	1st (?)	**Ewart Carvath (PoW)**
	11th	**Arthur Taverner**
	12th	**Harry Skelton**
	14th	**Oswald Elliott**

1917

March	20th – 21st	**George Atkinson; 20th William Close**
April	9th	Arras offensive begins
	12th	Canadians capture Vimy Ridge
	13th	**Maurice Wood**
	16th	Second Battle of Aisne begins
June	7th	Attack at Messines
	7th	**John Nowers**
	16th	**Cyril Clulee**
July	24th	**Herbert Leakey**
	31st	Battle of Passchendaele begins (lasts until 6th November)
	31st	**Charles Staplee**
August	27th	**Thomas Senescall**
September	6th	**George Murphy**
	30th	**Frank Davis**
October	12th	British offensive at Passchendaele
	20th	**Charles Beechey**
November		**Charles Branwhite (of wounds)**
December	3rd	**William Wass**
	24th	**Edward Smalley**
	29th	**Len Beechey**

1918

January	20th	**Herbert Jackson**
March	21st	German Spring Offensive begins Numerous conflicts around the Somme
	24th	**Walter Arnold**
	26th	**Seaforth Clarke**
April	14th	**John Andrews**
	24th	**George Clark**
May	27th	Third Battle of Aisne begins
	27th	**Henry Harrison**
June	5th	**William Markwick**
July	8th	**Arthur Claydon (MIA)**
	15th	Second Battle of Marne
August	8th	Amiens Offensive
	21st	Allied breakthrough at Albert
	22nd	**Ernest Hudson**
	25th	**Frederick Young**
September	13th	**John Parnwell Gray**
	18th	**Harry Curtis**
October	5th	Allied forces capture the Hindenburg Line
	17th	**Philip Thrower**
November	5th	**Cyril Leary**
	11th	Armistice signed

1919

August	10th	**Stanley Shepherd**

1924

April	29th	**Frank Healey**

The Lincolnshire Regiment in the First World War

By Rory Langan (OS)

The Lincolnshire Regiment started the war spread across Britain, and indeed th Empire, with the 1st Battalion being stationed in Portsmouth, the 2nd garrisonin Bermuda and the 4th and 5th spread throughout Lincolnshire with the 3rd Militia Battalio inactive. Over the course of the war 13 other battalions were raised but the 1st and 2nd, th core of the Regiment remained on the Western Front for the duration. Members o the Bermuda Volunteer Rifle Corps were also attached to the 1st Battalion and serve alongside them as an extra company. The Regiment's service consisted primarily o duties in the great charnel houses of the Western Front such as the Marne in 1914 Loos in 1915, the Somme in 1916, Passchendale and Cambrai in 1917, before final breaking through the Hindenburg Line in 1918. However, elements of the Regimer also stood in at the debacle at Gallipoli and did a tour of the Middle East in 1916.

The Regiment, and the Division that it was part of, the 46th North Midland, ca be considered, according to the historian Paddy Griffith[1], as one of the British Army's elit divisions on the Western Front, and this reputation is supported by its impressive list o battle honours that it picked up throughout the War:

Mons, Le Cateau, Retreat from Mons, Marne 1914, Aisne 1914, '18, La Bassée 1914 Messines 1914, 1917, 1918, Armentières 1914 Ypres 1914, '15, '17, Nonne Bosscher Neuve Chapelle, Gravenstafel, St. Julien, Frezenberg, Bellewaarde, Aubers, Loos, Somm 1916, '18, Albert 1916, '18, Bazentin, Delville Wood, Pozières, Flers-Courcelette, Morva Thiepval, Ancre 1916, '18, Arras 1917, '18, Scarpe 1917, '18, Arleux, Pilckem, Langemarc 1917, Menin Road, Polygon Wood, Broodseinde, Poelcappelle, Passchendaele, Cambra 1917, '18, St. Quentin, Bapaume 1918, Lys, Estaires, Bailleul, Kemmel, Amiens, Drocou Quéant, Hindenburg Line, Épéhy, Canal du Nord, St. Quentin Canal, Beaurevoir, Selle Sambre, France and Flanders 1914-18, Suvla, Landing at Suvla, Scimitar Hill, Gallipo 1915, Egypt 1916.

Not only this but three VCs were won by members of the Regiment, one of those a Gallipoli, won by Percy Howard Hansen, a Dane and only one of 14 VCs won by non Britis or Empire troops in its history.

[1]Griffith, Paddy *Battle Tactics of the Western Front – The British Army's Art of Attack 1916-191* Yale University Press (1996)

The action at the Hohenzollern Redoubt, 25th September – 15th October 1915

By Rory Langan (OS)

he Battle of the Hohenzollern Redoubt, (known to the Germans as the *ohenzollern Werk*) took place during the Battle of Loos near Auchy-les-Mines in France on ne Western Front in World War I. The British 9th Division captured the redoubt and then st it to a German counter-attack. The final British attempt to retake it on 13th October iled and resulted in heavy casualties, mostly in the first few minutes. The initial attack was d by troops of the Scottish 9th Division. Leading battalions from the 26th Brigade from the lack Watch, The Gordon Highlanders and the Argyll and Sutherland Highlanders advanced rough heavy machine gun fire, as well as gas fired from British guns which had failed o move with the wind into German trenches, before pausing to allow the British artillery e on the German trenches to finish. After this they advanced through withering German efensive fire and seized the German front lines running from "Mad" (Madagascar) trench n the left of the redoubt over to "Big Willie" and "The Dump" (a large slag pile from the gion's coal mining industry) on the extreme right. Further penetration into German lines own "Corons" trench proved difficult as retreating German troops opened a sluice which ooded the trench from knee to waist height.

owever, over the next week up until 3rd October counter-attacks by the German)th and 117th Divisions forced the Scots to pull back and the British Guards Division epped into the line to prevent the Germans gaining any ground. On 13th October the der was given to the 46th (North Midland) Division, a Territorial unit, to retake the edoubt. Men from the Lincolnshire, Leicestershire, Nottinghamshire and Staffordshire egiments moved into the line. After British artillery fired yet another cloud of fairly effective gas onto German lines, the 46th moved off, including the 4th and 5th ncolnshires, only to be met with even heavier fire than the Scottish troops were met with their initial attack. The 4th and 5th Lincolnshires were the first to go over the top; They ere wiped out in less then half an hour. The Division suffered over 3,500 casualties in ound the first minutes of the attack and was totally unable to penetrate the German wire hich had been repaired and was totally undamaged by British artillery.

his book *Tommy*, Richard Holmes cites a letter written by a Captain W. L. Weetman, ne of the few surviving officers of the Sherwood Foresters, to his superiors, describing e attempt to take the redoubt, in which the Hohenzollern Redoubt is described as "...*a ell known spot which you probably know of, though I think I had better leave it name- ss... of course they heard us coming and we knew it*". Weetman goes on to describe w most of his command was killed before reaching German lines and his commanding ficer was picked off by a sniper in the aftermath of the attack. All in all the attack was considered a bloody waste by both sides. In the British Official History, J. E. Edmonds wrote that *"The fighting [from 13–14 October] had not improved the general situation in any way and had brought nothing but useless slaughter of infantry"*. Casualties for the British amounted to 6,058 Scots of the 9th Division, 2,115 Guardsmen and 3,763 men of the Midlands Division. Of those killed, 90% of the 1/4th Lincolns and 97% of the 1/5th Lincoln have no known graves. The Germans had themselves suffered over 3,000 casualties over the course of the engagement.

The Commonwealth War Graves Commission

The CWGC was founded by Fabian Ware. He arrived in France in 1914 to command a British unit of the Red Cross. While there, he realised that there was no organisation in place to record the final grave locations of casualties. Concerned that graves may be lost forever, he commanded his unit to register and care for the graves that they could find. In 1915, he was given official recognition by the war office and his unit became known as the Graves Registration Committee. They received hundreds of requests from relatives for information and photographs, and by 1917 the committee had sent 12,000 photographs to relatives of the fallen.

Ware became convinced, as the war progressed, that an official organisation was needed to recognise the Imperial nature of the war and give equality to the treatment of the dead. In 1917, supported by the Prince of Wales, he submitted a memorandum to the Imperial War Commission. This led to the establishment of the Imperial War Graves Commission, which received a Royal Charter on 21st May 1917.

Three of the most famous architects of the time – Sir Edwin Lutyens, Sir Herbert Baker and Sir Reginald Blomfield – were chosen to design and construct the cemeteries and memorials. Three experimental cemeteries were constructed and the one in Forceville in France was deemed to be the most successful. It was a walled cemetery in a garden setting with uniformly designed headstones. It also included the Cross of Sacrifice designed by Blomfield to represent the faith of the majority, and the Stone of Remembrance, designed by Lutyens, to represent those of all faiths as well as those of none. Forceville was to be the template for the future construction programme.

Between 1923 and 1938, the Commission also had to construct numerous monuments to the missing. The largest was constructed in Thiepval. It stands over 45 metres high and is inscribed with the names of 72,000 casualties of the Battle of the Somme whose bodies were never found.

Each headstone was engraved with the soldier's regimental badge, rank, name, unit, date of death and, in some cases, an epitaph chosen by the next of kin is inscribed, as is the soldier's age. A firm in Lancashire designed a machine to trace the details onto each of the stones. Each cemetery was also planted with flowers and trees in order to soften the harshness of the rows of gravestones. The building programme began in 1919 and was not completed until 1938. The commission also worked tirelessly during the Second World War and continues to maintain the Commonwealth cemeteries that exist across the world.

The Cemetery Sites

Name	Cemetery	Reference
John Andrews	Aire Communal Cemetery	II. D. 12.
Walter Arnold	Pozières Memorial	Panel 90 to 93
George Atkinson	Plymouth (Ford Park) Cemetery	L. 25. 10.
Barnard Beechey	Ploegsteert Memorial	Panel 3.
Charles Beechey	Dar Es Salaam War Cemetery	6. E. 3
Len Beechey	St Sever Cemetery Extension	P.V.H. 12B
Charles Bird	Loos Memorial	Panel 31 – 34.
Albert Blades	Merville Communal Cemetery	XI A. 29
Charles Branwhite	Étaples Military Cemetery	XXX. M. 20A
George Clark	Pozières Memorial	Panel 81 - 84
Seaforth Clarke	Duisans British Cemetery	V.F. 24
Arthur Claydon	Caberet Rouge British Cemetery	VII. E.6
William Close	Arras Memorial	Bay 7
Cyril Clulee	Kandahar Farm Cemetery	II.B.22
Arthur Cowie	Dantzig Alley British Cemetery	VII. H.7
Albert Curtis	Varennes Military Cemetery	I.A.2
Harry Curtis	Dorian Military Cemetery	V.D.17
Horace Curtis	Helles Memorial	Panel 47 – 51
Frank Davis	Menin Gate	Addenda Panel 57
Oswald Elliott	Bécourt Military Cemetery	I.Y.15
Arthur Evans	Loos Memorial	Panel 31 - 34
Aubrey Glew	St Pierre Communal Cemetery	V.B.5
Charles Gray	Loos Memorial	Panel 31 - 34
John Gray	Stamford Cemetery	A.B.9
George Griffiths	Dar Es Salaam War Cemetery	Coll Grave 8. D. 1 – 4.
Victor-André Grivel	Munster Communal Cemetery	

Henry Harrison	Soissons Memorial	
Ernest Hudson	Vis en Artois Memorial	Panel 4
Herbert Jackson	Fins New British Cemetery	III. G. 12
Geoffrey Jones	Dantzig Alley	III. M. 10
Charles Knight	Lilliers Communal Cemetery	IV.C.54
Herbert Leakey	Dar Es Saleem War Cemetery	4.C.5
Cyril Leary	Bourne Cemetery	105.17
Charles Lowe	Vimy Memorial	
William Markwick	Peronne Communal Cemetery	V.M.9
George Murphy	Tyne Cot	Panel 22 – 28
John Nowers	Voormezelle Enclosure No.3	XIII. J. 21
Leonard Pitt	Birr Cross Roads Cemetery	I.E.36
Thomas Senescall	Hargicourt British Cemetery	I.C.18
Stanley Shepherd	Archangel Allied Cemetery	Sp.Mem. B 122
Harry Skelton	Heilly Station Cemetery	V.A.2
Edward Smalley	Templeux le Guerard	II.E.37
Harold Springthorpe	Helles Memorial	Panel 331
Charles Staplee	Menin Gate	Panels 6 – 8
Arthur Taverner	Grove Town Cemetery	I.B.1
Philip Thrower	Fresnoy le Grand Communal Cemetery Extension	A.21
William Wass	Gaza War Cemetery	XIII.E.2
Francis Whincup	Dartmoor Cemetery	I.E.35
Maurice Wood	Arras Flying Services Memorial	
William Wright	Arras Memorial	Bay 3 and 4
Frederick Young	Mailly Wood Cemetery	II.Q.1

Old Stamfordians lost to the First World War

John Alfred Raymond Andrews

2nd Lieutenant – Royal Air Force and 6th Battalion
– Lincolnshire Regiment

1896 – 1918

*"I need hardly tell you how sorry, not only myself, but the whole
squadron are at losing such a fine comrade, as during the time
he was with us he had become extremely popular, and was always
the first to volunteer for any dangerous work."*

Major R.E Paul, RAF, (BEF) in a letter to Fred Andrews
– reported by the Stamford Mercury, 1918.

John Alfred Raymond Andrews was born in Stamford in 1896, the son of Fred, a solicitor
clerk and his wife Ada Andrews (née Coverley). Fred and Ada were married in Spilsb
Lincolnshire in 1895. The family lived at 15A and later at 33 Adelaide Street in Stamfor
John attended the school from 1909 until 1911.

He was listed as Raymond on the 1901 and 1911 census records and had one sister, Ac
Phyllis Andrews, who was born in the town in 1899. Before the war, John worked as a bar
clerk and had also served with the Queen's Westminsters. He continued to serve with the:
after the outbreak of war in 1914. He fought for this regiment on the Somme where he wa
recommended for a commission.

hn was promoted to the rank of 2nd Lieutenant in the 6th Battalion Lincolnshire
egiment in 1917. In the same year, he was also given a further commission and
ansferred to the Royal Flying Corps which would become the Royal Air Force on
pril 1st 1918.

e was killed on 14th April 1918 while working as an observer for the No. 4 Squadron
' the RAF. He was flying with Lieutenant Albert Edward Doughty (MM).

ney are both buried in Aire Communal Cemetery in France. It was reported in the
ercury in May 1918 that his death was instantaneous and had *"hit the flight very badly"*.
also noted in this report that he was a qualified observer.

ne day of his death was reportedly a misty day with rain and low cloud cover, which may
ave affected visibility conditions from the plane.

AF observers were mainly used for reconnaissance missions and, until 1917, they did not
eceive much in the way of formal training. Most observers would also be able to control
ie aircraft.

hn was just 21 years old when he died. He left £161 2s 5d to his mother, Ada. His father
ed in 1937, aged 79, and his mother died in 1962. His sister, Ada died in Stamford in 1993.

Walter Clay Arnold

Lance Corporal – 20th Battalion
– Machine Gun Corps (Infantry) (86414)
1883 – 1918

"Our life for yours" (Joshua 11.14)

The entrance to the Pozieres British Cemetery where
Walter Clay Arnold is commemorated

Walter Clay Arnold was born in 1883 in Saxilby, Lincolnshire. He was the son of the Bourn
Chief of Police, Charles Arnold, and his wife, Mary. Walter attended Stamford School from
1898 until 1899. He had three older siblings – Sarah, born c. 1880, Ethel born c. 1881 and
Charles, born c. 1882.

At the start of 1911, Walter married Edith Mary (née Cross) in Melton Mowbray. Edith was
born in Stamford in August 1882. They lived at 135 Hadfield Street in Sheffield where Walter
was working as a pawnbroker manager. The couple had one son, Geoffrey Norman Arnold
who was born in April 1913.

Walter joined up in December 1915 and served with the Training Reserve Battalion and was
appointed to the rank of Lance Corporal in the Machine Gun Corps in December 1917. He
was admitted to hospital in July 1917 and killed in action on 24th March 1918, in one of
the final battles of the Somme. This conflict started on March 21st and ended on July 4th.

The Battle of the Somme in 1918 comprised a series of battles along the Somme river.
The German forces were able to make some significant ground during this campaign and
this forced the allies to re-evaluate their command structure. Walter was aged 34 at the
time of his death. He had served for 2 years and 106 days. He has no known grave and is
commemorated on the Pozières Memorial which is located on the Somme.

Walter's son, Geoffrey, served with the RAF in World War Two and died on 19th August
1941 on the HMS Aguila which is believed to have been sunk by a torpedo while in a convoy
to Gibraltar. He is commemorated on the Runnymede Memorial in Surrey. He left £312 16
to his mother. She died in 1950.

George Louis Atkinson

Captain – Royal Army Medical Corps

1867– 1917

The hospital ship on which George was serving at the time of his death,

*"So far as outward signs would indicate, she was
still full of sick and wounded"*

New York Times report on the sinking of the Hospital Ship,
Asturias March 28th 1917.

eorge Atkinson was born in Lambeth in early 1867. In 1881, he was living at 2 St Leonard's Street, Stamford with his parents, Eloisa and George, his grandmother loisa Barston and his brothers, Arthur (born c. 1869), Eustace (born c. 1871) and erbert (born c. 1880) and his sisters, Helen (born c. 1872), Kate (born c. 1876) and Eloisa orn c. 1878). His father was an artist and clay modeller who died in 1913, his mother ied in 1929.

eorge attended Stamford School from 1876 until 1886. He appears to have been both cademic and sporty. In 1886, he came second in the quarter mile (open) race at Sports ay and came first in the lacrosse race. He also passed the London Matriculation Exam the First Division. George served as secretary for the school athletic and cricket club the general meeting of 1886. He also played both football and cricket for the school.

fter leaving school, he obtained a Mastership at Sale College, Manchester and terwards he was a Warneford Scholar at King's College, London where he became M.R.C.S Member of the Royal College of Surgeons) and L.R.C.P. (Licentiate of the Royal College of hysicians). He then acted as House Surgeon at King's College Hospital for Children.

Vhen war broke out, George was working as a doctor and living in Hampton Hill, London ith his wife Florence (née Russell), whom he married in Plymouth in 1898. They had a aughter, Joyce who was born in Surrey in 1902.

George took a temporary commission as Lieutenant in the Royal Army Medical Corps 1914 and was promoted to Captain a year later.

He drowned on the hospital ship Asturias between 20th and 21st March, 1917 and buried in Ford Park Cemetery in Devon.

The Asturias had been involved in numerous crossings from France, bringing th wounded back from the Western Front. She had room for 896 patients but often carrie many more. The ship also served in the Eastern Mediterranean during the Dardenelle campaign.

The Argus Newspaper from Melbourne, Victoria notes that the Asturias wa torpedoed by a German submarine. The ship had no patients aboard at the time, havin previously docked at Avonmouth. The newspaper states that two torpedoes struck the ship a midnight on March 20th while the majority of staff and crew were in bed.

She sank around 5 miles off Start Point in Devon. The New York Times of March 28th 191 notes that 31 people were killed in the incident. It was reported that, outwardly, the shi appeared to be carrying the wounded and, as such, the sinking of the ship was considere to be a shocking event. The remaining hulk of the ship was used as a floating ammunitio store for the rest of the war.

George's daughter, Joyce, married John Barradale in 1940 and died in 1990 on the Isle c Wight.

The Beechey Brothers

"It was no sacrifice ma'am, I did not give them willingly"

Amy Beechey in response to Queen Mary's thanks for her sacrifice, April 1918.

everend Prince William Thomas Beechey was appointed to be Rector of Friesthorpe, incoln in 1890. By that time, he and his wife, Amy (née Reeve) had already suffered the oss of a child, a daughter named Maud, who died aged 5 in 1885. She was their third child, orn after Barnard (1877) and Charles (1878).

n total, Amy would give birth to 14 children between the years of 1877 and 1899 and the ev. Beechey would often struggle to remember the names of his many offspring, repeating he names in birth order like a nursery rhyme until he found the correct one!

etween 1911 and the end of the Great War, Amy would lose her husband and five of er sons and see another son permanently disabled. Three of the five sons that Amy lost ad direct connections with Stamford School. Barnard, known as Bar, Charles, known s Char and Leonard or Len all appear on the memorial in the school chapel, as well as ppearing, with their brothers, Frank and Harold, on a marble plaque in St Peter's Church, riesthorpe, where the family had moved to in 1890.

everend Beechey died on May 5th 1912 of cancer. His illness had meant the family had loved from the Rectory at Friesthorpe to a smaller house at 14 Avondale Street, Lincoln. .my Beechey would move again, to 197 Wragby Road in Lincoln, and it would be here that he would receive news of her sons' deaths.

lore information on the Beechey Brothers can e found in Michael Walsh's *Brothers in War*.

Barnard Reeve Beechey

Sergeant – 9th Lincolnshire Regiment (13773)

1877 – 1915

*"I really am all right and don't mind the life, only
we all wish the thing was over"*

Barnard Beechey in a letter – written in September 1915
(he was killed on 25th September 1915)

Barnard Beechey was a maths teacher at Stamford School from 1899 until 1901. He was born in Pinchbeck, Lincolnshire in 1877. He was the eldest of the Beechey children and the first of the brothers to be killed.

Bar was educated at St John's Foundation School for the Sons of Poor Clergy, where he held a scholarship, and then at Leatherhead. He then won an Open Exhibition to join St John's College, Cambridge. After leaving employment at Stamford School, he became mathematics master at the grammar school at Wotton Under Edge in Gloucestershire and after that he worked as Deputy Headmaster at Dorchester Grammar School. He is listed there in the 1911 census.

While at Stamford, Beechey is noted as having played football for the staff v Peterborough masters on October 4th 1900 and against Uppingham Town on October 7th but the team suffered a heavy 7 – 0 defeat in both of these matches!

At Dorchester Grammar, he was known as a very knowledgeable teacher but was also known for his unpredictable temper. He set up the Officer Training Corps and ran the first XI football team (as his brother Charles did at Stamford). He left the school in June 1912.

y the time war was declared, Bar was employed by the local education authority and living
home in Lincoln with his widowed mother. His promising career seemed to have faltered
omewhat and he was possibly keen to prove himself by joining up when war was declared
1914.

e joined the 9th Lincolns as a private (an unpaid debt to the military for his OTC uniform
ayed as a blight on his record and meant that he could not enter as a higher rank despite
is high academic qualifications) but he was quickly promoted to the rank of Sergeant.

arnard Beechey was killed on 25th September 1915, the first day of the Battle of Loos,
ged 38. He had been at the front for only a few weeks.

he Battle of Loos was the largest conflict that the BEF had been involved in by 1915.
5,000 men would take part in the battle. The aim was to reach the German rear lines and
ake control of their communications, perhaps even causing them to retreat. It involved
front of 25 miles and this meant that ammunition was stretched far beyond its means.
some areas, the battle was very successful but other areas struggled due to lack of
ommunication. Ultimately, the Battle of Loos was unsuccessful as reserve divisions were
o far away to consolidate any gains that the allies had achieved in the early hours of the
onflict. The battle ended on September 28th.

my Beechey kept a photograph of her son's grave – a plain wooden cross – until the day
ne died. It is likely that this cross was put up either as a memorial in the area that he died
r that the grave was lost at a later date, possibly during future battles in the area.

oday, no known grave exists and his name is inscribed on the Ploegsteert memorial to the
nissing in Belgium.

Charles Reeve Beechey

Private – 25th Battalion – Royal Fusiliers (58708)

1878 – 1917

"These last three years seem so awful to us after the 20 we spent in such peace and enjoyment, so let me now hope that we have had our share of the losses although we are taking more than our share of the dangers."

A letter to his mother after the death of his brother, Frank, written in the trenches at Agny, 1916.

For seven years from 1890, 'Char' Beechey was a boarding pupil at Stamford Schoo During this time, he would have studied Latin and Greek six mornings a week and maths o four afternoons and would have lived in a room in what is now School House and the RLC During his schooldays, he played football and cricket for the school, and academically h excelled at mathematics, which he would later return to the school to teach.

Charles Reeve Beechey was born in Pinchbeck, Lincolnshire in April 1878. After leavin the school in 1897, he followed his older brother, Barnard, and took a place at St John College, Cambridge where he played for the University firsts in football. He joined th school staff as a maths teacher in May 1913 after teaching at three other schools.

At Stamford, now as a master, he established a photographic club and a natural histor society and he ran the first XI football team (as his brother, Barnard did at Dorchester Grammar School).

Charles stayed at the school even when his brothers and many other staff member joined up in the early days of the war. When he received the telegram from his mothe informing him of his brother Barnard's death in 1915, he was in the middle of teachin a class. He read the telegram and put it away in his pocket. It was only at the end of th lesson that Mr Beechey told his class the news and then went to see the Headmaster and as permission to return to the family home in Lincoln.

ventually, the pressure that he must have felt at not being in service took its toll and he oined up. He served as a Private in the 25th Battalion, Royal Fusiliers and fought on the omme.

harles carried a miniature chess set with him for entertainment in the trenches. He also eceived copies of the Stamford Mercury and in a letter to his mother on 12th October 916, he writes home as follows:

" see by the last (edition of the newspaper) that another of our Stamford Old Boys as been killed, one of the Glews, an aviator whom Bar saw fly at Horncastle".

is interest in the boys and the school that he had left behind was evident and he eturned regularly while on leave from the trenches.

e became ill while in France and was sent to recover at a hospital in Birmingham and later o convalesce in Surrey. By May 1917, he was stationed at a barracks in Dover when he rote a letter stating that *"I missed the train at Stamford through staying on the cricket eld too long"*; he had returned to school to play cricket for the staff and had to quickly earrange his journey back to Dover.

he cricket games were not to last, however, and he sailed from Plymouth in July 1917 to e-join the Fusiliers who were now posted in East Africa. There appears to be a huge sense f relief in his letters that he was not returning to the trenches and a feeling that he may be little safer in Africa. He also felt that the climate would be much better for him. In Africa, harles was also able to indulge his constant love of natural history, noting the beauty of the ative butterflies and the oddness of the trees, flora and fauna. But the peace and relative afety that he and indeed his family felt was to be short lived.

n 20th October 1917, Lieutenant H.M Peacock wrote to Amy Beechey to inform her that er second son had been injured. Charles was in a field hospital suffering from a bullet ound to his chest. He died later that day.

e had suffered fatal machine gun wounds. His best friend, Private P Heath, wrote to anon Day from his own hospital bed in Africa. In this letter, Private Heath notes that harles was suffering from sickness when they had reached the front line. He had gone o get more ammunition from the reserve lines and was struck in the chest by machine un fire. Heath also states that Charles, a teacher to the end, carried his chess set and a ompass so that he would always be able to know where he was. He also notes that often, ne men would crowd around this compass to learn their whereabouts. Heath goes on to ympathise with Canon Day and the boys who had suffered the loss of their schoolmaster.

eechey's death meant that all of Canon Day's August 1914 staff had been killed in action.

harles was 39 at the time of his death and is buried in Dar es Salaam War Cemetery, anzania. This was on the site of the No. 3 East African Stationary Hospital.

harles Beechey left a sum of money in his will to the school which was used for the eechey Cup. This was awarded for many years to the best fielder of the cricket season.

Leonard Reeve Beechey

18th Battalion – London Regiment
(London Irish Rifles) (593763)

1881 – 1917

*"My darling mother, don't feel like doing much yet.
Lots of love, Len"*

Leonard Beechey in spidery handwriting – the last words he wrote.

Leonard Beechey was born on 31st August 1881 in Southwark, London. He attended th
school in 1897, the year his brother Charles left. Before that, Leonard had attended Christ
Hospital School, Lincoln, along with his other brother, Chris.

After leaving school, Len worked as a clerk for a Railway Clearing House. He was marrie
to Frances Smith, a widow, known to the rest of his family as 'Annie'. They were marrie
on 15th November 1915 but his family did not attend as they believed the couple had bee
married for many years already!

He joined up in 1916 and served as a Rifleman.

Len regularly wrote home from the trenches and a number of his letters from 1917 show
a hope that his brother, Charles, was safe in his posting in East Africa and missing th
dangers of trench life.

When he hears of Charles' death in 1917, he is unable to put into words anything to hel
his mother and says simply in a letter on 3rd November

"it seems such a great pity that he should have to go".

n November 7th, he writes a little more, stating:

ach one seems a harder blow than the previous one. I wish I could see you".

e knew how much Stamford School had meant to his elder brother and in a letter to his
ster Edith, he says

*am glad that he left a cup for Stamford School as he was connected with it for such
long time. I think he went there when we first got to Friesthorpe, which is about
3 years ago."*

en was gassed and wounded at Bourlon Wood and his mother received a letter on 10th
ecember 1917 from the Army Chaplain, Stanley Hide. He was informing her that her son
as in hospital. Enclosed with that letter was a brief scrawled note from Len, written on
h December. These would be the last words he wrote.

e died on 29th December 1917 of tetanus bacteria and is buried in St. Sever Cemetery
xtension in Rouen.

Charles Goodeve Bird

Lance Corporal – 4th Battalion
– Lincolnshire Regiment D Company (2466)

1882 – 1915

"Should have made many more runs."

Stamfordian, Christmas 1900. Characters of the XI.

Charles Goodeve Bird was born in the autumn of 1882 to Albert, an agent for a co
company, and Sarah Louisa Bird (née Goodeve). He enlisted in the Stamford Territoria
and fell along with Arthur Evans, Charles Gray and Charles Knight at the Hohenzolle
Redoubt in October 1915.

During his time at the school, he regularly played in the cricket team and th
Stamfordian of Christmas 1900 notes that he *"kept wicket fairly successfully but was rath
disappointing in his batting"*. He left the school at Easter 1901. In the 1901 censu
Charles is listed as an Agricultural Engineer Apprentice but is also a patient at the Stamfo
Infirmary on Wharf Road.

His parents lived at 46 St Martin's, Stamford, at the time of their son's death. The Stamfo
Mercury reported on October 30th 1915 that he was in hospital but this was not offici
news and his exact whereabouts were unclear.

It wasn't until December that official notice was received that Charles had been killed
action two months previously.

He has no known grave and is commemorated on the Loos Memorial. He left £158 11s
to his father, Albert in his will.

Albert Moisey Blades

Lance Corporal – Royal Berkshire Regiment (6004)

1895 –1916

"I know you will be proud of his heroic memory"

Regimental Chaplain writing to his parents
– quoted in The Stamfordian, Christmas 1916.

Albert Moisey Blades was born in Stamford in 1895. He was the second son of Tom and Ellen Blades (née Hibbitt). His father worked as a newspaper clerk. He had two brothers, Frederick (born c. 1891) and Francis (born c. 1899). The family had lived on the Casterton Road in a house named 'Shamrock Villa'.

Albert was at the school only briefly, leaving in 1909. He then went to work as a clerk for 'Messrs. Phipps of Scotgate'. Phipps was a well-known brewery company from Northampton that also had premises in Stamford.

The 7th Battalion of the Essex Regiment were billeted to Stamford in December 1914 and Albert joined up with them. He was transferred later into the Royal Berkshire Regiment. He served with the 2/4th Battalion which landed at Le Havre on 27th May 1916.

Albert was badly wounded on July 19th 1916, probably during the first day of the Battle of Fromelles, and his leg was shattered. It is noted in the Stamfordian of Christmas 1916 that despite the best of efforts of the medical staff he died from his wounds just four days later.

The Battle of Fromelles lasted for only two days and was an attempt to prevent the German forces from moving troops out of the area to contest the Battle of the Somme.

It was also hoped that they may have been forced to relocate some troops from the Somme to the area around Fromelles. It is generally thought that, due to the resources and intelligence being used on the Somme campaign, the Battle of Fromelles was a poorly planned campaign. The Germans were expecting the attack and manned their machine guns in advance of the assault. Many of the dead or wounded were left lying in no man's land until the attack was over. It is considered the worst 24 hours in Australian military history – 5,533 men from the Australian 5th Division were killed, wounded or reported missing in just one night.

At the time of his death, Albert's parents were living at 25 Houston Road, Brownsover in Rugby. His father died in January 1934 aged 68 and his mother died in June 1960 aged 93. They are buried in the Clifton Road cemetery in Rugby and Albert is also commemorated on their grave stone. It is noted that he *"died from enemy action, July 1916"*. The stone was put up by his brothers.

Albert is buried in the Merville Communal Cemetery in Northern France. Merville served as a hospital station from 1915 – 1918.

His brother, Francis, served with the Worcestershire Regiment and survived the war, dying in 1993.

Charles Evelyn Branwhite (MM)

Lance Corporal – 7th Battalion C.E.F.
– 1st British Columbia Regiment (116137)

1884 –1917

His original grave marker.

"For conspicuous gallantry and devotion to duty…"

Military medal citation, March 1918.

The youngest son of Charles, a wine and spirit agent, and his wife, Ellen Mary Branwhite, Charles Branwhite was born in Lowestoft, Suffolk on 28th October 1884. He had two brothers, Harry (born c. 1874) and William (born c. 1875) and a sister, Ethel (born c. 1876). He attended Stamford School from 1900 to 1903. During this time, he was awarded the School House prize for Divinity in 1901 and in the same year, he was involved in the Debating Society. On October 15th, he proposed "That the Navy has been of more use than the Army" winning this debate by 6 votes to 4!

Charles was also involved in the hurdles race of the 1901 Sports Day and captained the first XI football team in 1902. It was noted that he was *"A thoroughly hardworking and conscientious captain, though heavily handicapped through lack of weight and pace.* He also played for the cricket team during his time at school.

He emigrated to Canada in 1906 and found work as a farmer. Charles enlisted in Vancouver in 1915 at the age of 30. In a letter to his brother on October 25th 1914, he says that,

"it seems to me to be almost my duty to go, as had I still been in England there is no doubt I should have enlisted, and because I happen to be out here, should not, I think, be any excuse for shirking my duty".

Charles died of wounds sustained at the Passchendaele Ridge in November 1917. In the action that led to his death, Charles behaved with such gallantry that he was recommended for a Military Medal, which was awarded posthumously on 13th March 1918.

He was 33 years old when he was killed. The form that lists the circumstances of his death reads as follows:

"This non-commissioned officer was wounded in the leg by a bullet, early in the attack on November 10th. He remained in the line until the company was relieved, when he was sent out to No.26 General Hospital, Étaples, where he succumbed to his wounds".

He is buried in Étaples Military Cemetery in France. This area was quite a distance from the front line and therefore was host to many hospital and casualty clearing bases.

By November 1917, Passchendaele Ridge was heavily armed with German soldiers – many who had left the Eastern Front had been sent to defend this important area. However, the allies still managed to take the village of Passchendaele on November 6th.

Ewart Blake Carvath

Private – 10th Battalion – Middlesex Regiment
(2024/290442)

1887 – 1916

"Died while Prisoner of War. Cause of death not given"

Notice in his Service Record. 1916.

wart Carvath was the son of James and Florence Marshall Carvath (née Blake) from Bourne. e had two brothers (Herbert born c. 1886 and Roy born c.1897) and three sisters (Lillian rn c. 1883, Gladys born c.1890 and Marjorie born c. 1894). He was born in Devon but the nily lived for a time on North Street, Bourne. His father was a Baptist minister.

wart attended the school from Christmas 1901 until Midsummer 1903. He is mentioned in ootball team for the school versus Deacon's in February 1903. By 1911, he was working a draper's assistant in Grantham.

e joined up on 11th August 1914, giving his address as 52 King's Street, Hammersmith. s place of enlistment was Stamford Brook Lodge in Middlesex. He served with the 2nd orfolk Regiment from October 1914 until May 1915 before re-joining the 10th Battalion the Middlesex Regiment. He died while a Prisoner of War at the start of October 1916 he cause of death was not given.

e had served for 2 years and 82 days. His personal effects were returned to his father at his dress in North Street, Bourne. His sister Gladys acknowledged receipt of his war medals July 1918. His brother, Roy, served with the Machine Gun Corps and survived the war, coming a dentist, and dying in 1978 in Bourne. It is not known where Ewart is buried.

s father died in 1929 and his mother in 1933.

George Herbert Clark

Rifleman – 2nd Battalion – Rifle Brigade (40885)

1899 – 1918

*"Clark broke away and scored with a neat oblique
shot from the right wing."*

2nd Team football report on match v. Laxton (away) Stamfordian Summer 1915.

George Clark was born in Stamford in 1899 and lived with his parents, Sam and Ro[...]
(née Bland) who were married in Kilburn, Middlesex in 1897. Sam worked for a brewe[...]
company as a salesman. The family lived at 3 Brownlow Terrace and George was their on[...]
child. He attended the school from January 1913 until April 1916.

In 1913, George appeared in the school production of Twelfth Night, playing the part [...]
Sebastian. He also played both football and cricket for the school. He was awarded 2n[...]
team football colours and in his final Sports Day in 1916, he came 2nd in the high jump an[...]
also won the quarter mile open race. He also served with the School Cadet Corps.

George joined up in London and served firstly with the London Regiment and then with th[...]
2nd Battalion Rifle Brigade.

He was killed in action on 24th April 1918 probably during the spring offensives that we[...]
designed to break the deadlock of the war.

He has no known grave and is commemorated on the Pozières Memorial. Walter Cl[...]
Arnold appears on the same memorial, just a few panels away.

Seaforth St John Clarke

Private – 2nd Battalion – Seaforth Highlanders (204640)

1898 –1918

Clarke was the only batsman who made a good score for the boarders"

Cricket report, Stamfordian, Christmas 1915.

aforth Clarke was born in 1898 in Surrey, the son of Hugh St John Clarke, an insurance d mortgage broker and his wife, Florence Meira Zelia Stewart Mackenzie, whose father as Colonel Keith William Stewart Mackenzie, who was born in Scotland. Seaforth had one ster, Moulie, born in about 1900. Florence died in 1912. Hugh would die in 1933.

aforth's address in probate was given as 19 Colinette Road, Putney and his father was ted as an accountant. The Stamfordian of Spring 1915 states that:

is interesting to note that S. St. J.Clarke, who joined the School this term, is a andson of an Old Stamfordian (1835-39), the Rev. J. S. Clarke, of Goudhurst, Kent, scholar of the School eighty years ago, under the Rev. F. E. Gretton."

ev James Sanderson Clarke died in 1911 at the Vicarage in Goudhurst. He had attended mbridge University, joining in 1839, before marrying Annie Pitt in Putney in 1865. The uple had 10 children, one of whom was Hugh St John Clarke.

aforth was playing for the school cricket XI in 1916 and it is noted that he:

as increased his scoring powers but has lost some of his powers of defence. t up too many catches by ill timed strokes on leg side. Capital field at point."

e was Lance Corporal in the School Cadet Corps in 1916 and was awarded school cricket ours in 1915.

aforth enlisted in Kingston-upon-Thames, Surrey, in 1917, joining the Seaforth ghlanders, possibly due to his maternal family connections in Ross and Cromarty, where e regiment was based. He was killed in action on 26th March 1918 and is buried in isans British Cemetery in France, 9km west of Arras. This area was used as a casualty aring centre until April 1918. The majority of burials in this cemetery are casualties from e battle of Arras in 1918.

Arthur Claydon (D.F.C)

32nd Squadron – RFC/RAF

1885 – 1918

"Recently this officer, single handed, went to the assistance of another pilot who was attacked… By his gallant conduct and skilful manoeuvring he not only extricated the pilot but drove down several of the enemy aeroplanes"

DFC citation, London Gazette, 1918.

In 1916, Arthur Claydon was working as a general contractor and living in Winnipe Manitoba. He enlisted on 18th February 1916 and joined the Canadian Field Artille His brother, Ernest Claydon (born c. 1894) also enlisted in Winnipeg and served with t Imperial Mechanical Transport Division and later with the Royal Naval Air Service.

Arthur had three other brothers, Ebenezer (born. c. 1880), Benjamin (born. c. 1882) a Cecil (born. c.1889). The family had emigrated to Canada in 1911.

After serving with an artillery regiment, Arthur transferred to the Royal Flying Corps 1917 and was posted to 32 Squadron later that year. This squadron was formed in 1916 a fighter unit, flying numerous patrols across the Western Front.

Born in Deeping St James on 25th September 1885, he was the son of Benjamin Robe Claydon, a mariner in the merchant service, and his wife, Annie Kitchen, who was also bc in Deeping St James.

st XI Football 1915-16

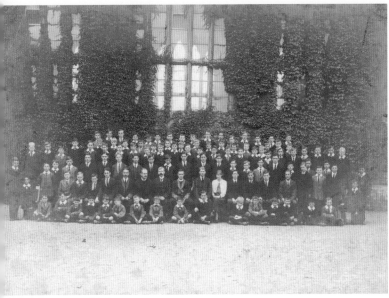

School House 1914

Arthur Claydon and
friends, Vendome, 1918
(Page 42)

Stanley Le Fleming
Shepherd (Page 86)

CCF 1916

School House 1918

St Mary's Hill, home of
Charles Shortland Gray
and John Parnwell Gray
(Page 61-62)

52 High Street, St Martins, home
of Geoffrey Jones (Page 69)

38 St Mary's Street, home of Henry Harrison (Page 65)

11 Ironmonger Street, home of Arthur Evans (Page 57)

PARISH OF ST MARTIN' STAMFORD BARON
WITH WOTHORPE
IN GRATEFUL MEMORY OF THE MEN WHO GAVE THEIR
LIVES FOR THEIR COUNTRY IN THE GREAT WAR 1914-1918

CAPT. M. HISSEY
LT. H. K. B. NEVINSON
SERGT. E. PALMER
L. CPL. C. G. BIRD
L. CPL. R. J. HENNESSEY
A. B. H. WATSON
GNR. C. E. TAYLOR
SPR. P. H. THROWER M.M.
SERGT. J. WRIGHT
PTE. G. BETTS
PTE. R. G. BETTS
PTE. J. BRANSTON
PTE. L. CORNELL
PTE. L. CROSS

PTE. F. CROWTHER
PTE. D. CUFF
PTE. W. H. GOODLIFFE
PTE. C. G. HAYNE
PTE. B. INGRAM
PTE. C. JAMES
PTE. A. LAWLESS
PTE. J. LENTON
PTE. A. S. LENTON
PTE. A. M. MARKS
PTE. G. NICKERSON
PTE. J. NICHOLLS
PTE. J. K. PEPPER

PTE. J. ROBINSON
PTE. H. SHELVEY
PTE. H. SMITH
PTE. R. STANGAR
PTE. C. STEELE
PTE. J. STRATTON
PTE. J. THOMPSON
PTE. F. C. THURRELL
PTE. B. WALTHAM
PTE. A. WATSON
PTE. O. WILLIAMS
PTE. F. WOODS
PTE. S. T. B. WOODWARD

"THEIR NAME LIVETH FOR EVERMORE"

Memorial on the outer wall of
St Martin's Church, Stamford

(L-R) The Victory Medal,
The 1914 – 15 Star, The
British War Medal.

1914 · 1918

THE ROOD IS DEDICATED
TO ALMIGHTY GOD IN
THANKSGIVING FOR
VICTORY AND PEACE
AND IN HONOURED MEMORY
OF LIVES LAID DOWN·

GEORGE HERBERT CLARK
CHARLES COOK
CHARLES SHORTLAND GRAY
JOHN PARNWELL GRAY
ARTHUR HENRY JOSEPH HOLLIS
ARTHUR INGLE
WILLIAM INGLIS JOHNSON
HARRY GORDON MASON
WILLIAM GEORGE MINTON
JOHN ANTHONY NOWERS
WILLIAM ARTHUR SAVAGE
HAROLD THOMAS SPRINGTHORPE
WILLIAM RICHARDSON WRIGHT
HARRY FOSTER LAVENDER

Memorial Plaque in
St Mary's Church, Stamford

The War Memorial, Stamford

Year 9 boys learn about Arthur Claydon.
Caberet Rouge Cemetery. April 2014.

Caberet Rouge Cemetery, resting place of Arthur Claydon. Taken in 1937. (Page 42

Grave of Arthur Cowie.
Dantzig Alley Cemetery, Mametz (Page 46)

Grave of Albert Curtis.
Varennes Military Cemetery (Page 49)

Becourt Cemetery. The resting place of Oswald Elliott (Page 55)

The grave of Oswald Elliott. Becourt (Page 55)

Heilly Station Cemetery. Resting place of Harry Skelton (Page 88)

thur joined the school at Michaelmas 1899 and left in 1901. During his time at the school, e appears to have excelled at mathematics. The Stamfordian notes that he completed the division maths paper *"near perfectly"* and was awarded the prize for mathematics in 001. He also obtained one of the highest marks in the geography paper of that year, along ith two other boys from the same form group – form III.

e was shot down by the Bavarian ace Max von Müller on 11th November 1917 but rvived this crash. He scored his first victory while flying the D.H.5, a single seat fighter rcraft with a forward firing machine gun which had made its first flight in August 1916.

May and June of 1918, Arthur scored six more victories flying the S.E.5a which was a plane fighter, introduced in March 1917.

rthur was reported as missing in action on 8th July 1918. He was seen at around 8.30am at morning chasing three enemy aircraft before being hit and steering his plane towards e ground. His aircraft was spotted on the ground the next day by his comrades from e air.

e had been shot down by Paul Billik, a famous German ace of the Prussian regiment, Jasta 2. He was awarded the Distinguished Flying Cross on 3rd August 1918.

rthur was buried in the Caberet Rouge British Cemetery in Souchez. This cemetery is amed after the Caberet Rouge café that was once situated on the site.

letter from his brother, Ben, discusses the circumstances of Arthur's death. He says:

?oor old boy, it hurts me to write, but at last we ive the facts. His machine... was shot down... uth of Lille and between Sechin and Carvin. e was dead when the machine came down and was uried as a British Pilot, Captain, name nknown... In despair of getting from our own uthorities, I tried the Huns and with success."

e goes on to state that a German acquaintance of a iend of his had said that Arthur

lied the death of a hero in his country's service".

e also notes his intention to go to France and visit e grave.

rthur's nephew, the son of his brother benezer, was named David Arthur Claydon. le was born in 1921 in Winnipeg. He served s a pilot for the Royal Canadian Airforce WW2 and was killed in January 1944. He is uried at Charlottenburg, Berlin.

Gravestone of Arthur Claydon.
Caberet Rouge Cemetery

William Colin Close

2nd Lieutenant – 3rd/6th Battalion – Northamptonshire Regiment

1897 – 1917

"He was deservedly popular with all ranks, being a good soldier and leader of men. He was much loved by the men and highly esteemed by his brother officers."

Regimental Colonel, 1917.

William was born in Collyweston in 1897, the son of Robert Henry, a farmer and slater, an his wife, Emma (née Collins). The family lived at The Poplars, New Road, Collyweston an later at Geeston House in Ketton.

William joined the school in September 1906. During his time at school, he won colou in both football and rugby and was a member of the Cadet Corps. He also attende Wellingborough School.

William had a brother, Geoffrey (born c. 1900) and a sister, Monica, (born c. 1903).

On 20th September 1915, he was promoted (on probation) to 2nd Lieutenant in th Northamptonshire Regiment and went to the front in August 1916. He was killed b machine gun fire while on reconnaissance on 20th March 1917, aged 20.

He is commemorated on the Arras Memorial. He is also commemorated on the Collywesto War Memorial. His war medals were sent to his father at Geeston House in Ketton.

Cyril Shakespeare Clulee

Gunner – New Zealand Field Artillery (2/857)

1894 – 1917

"Our Glorious Dead"

Inscription on the Southampton Cenotaph. Cyril is commemorated on this memorial.

yril Clulee was born in Aston, Warwickshire in spring 1894, the last child of banker Harry rthur and his wife, May (née Trotter). His mother died in 1903 and his father in 1907. He ad a sister, Dorothy, who was born c. 1889 and a brother, Harold who was born c. 1887. he family lived at 189 High Street, Aston and later on Heath Mill Lane also in Aston.

yril joined the school at Midsummer 1904. He received a form prize in 1905 and again 1906. He was also awarded The Welby Prize and the School House Prize for Divinity in 905.

e emigrated to Sydney in 1911 and enlisted on 26th October 1914, aged 20. On nlistment, his address was given as Mount Eden Road, Auckland, New Zealand and he ave his occupation as 'farm hand'.

1 January 1915, he was serving in Egypt. He was wounded in September and again in ovember 1916. Cyril was promoted to the rank of Bombardier after a campaign in Egypt 1 January 1915 and further promoted to acting Corporal on 24th January 1917.

e was killed in action on 16th June 1917 and is buried in Kandahar Farm Cemetery in elgium. He was 23.

e left £200 in his will to his maternal aunt, Ida Trotter, a spinster and his next of kin who lso received his campaign medals and lived in Hampshire. His name also appears on the outhampton Cenotaph.

Arthur William Spring Cowie

2nd Lieutenant – 7th Battalion – Lincolnshire Regiment

1886 – 1916

"He was one of the sincerest, truest and most loyal men that I ever had the privilege of knowing and he had that rare gift of being able to judge a boy's character... a truer man never stepped".

John Duncan Day – Christmas 1916 – Stamfordian

Arthur Cowie's inspiration was such that one of his pupils, Aubrey Glew, noted when he had killed another pilot that he had finally *"avenged Cowie's death"*. It is said that numerous Stamfordians joined up to fight after the inspirational Mr Cowie was killed in 1916.

Born in Bengal, India on 8th March 1886, Arthur was the youngest son of Henry George Cowie and his wife Sophia Jane Campbell Court from Tiverton in Devon. His father, who worked for the Indian Financial Department, died in 1903 and his mother in 1906. The family had lived at 4 Old Blundells in Tiverton and Arthur attended Blundell's School from the age of 12 as a day boy. He was a member of the Blundell's OTC from 1900 until 1904.

Arthur had seven siblings – Helen (born. c. 1870), Henry (born and died 1872), Henry (born c. 1872), Charles (born. c. 1875), David (born.c.1878), Agnes (born. c. 1880) and Mary (born. c. 1882).

rthur Cowie joined Stamford School in 1912 as a master of Classics. He had previously
een a Classics scholar at Balliol College, Oxford.

hile at Stamford, he was a keen sportsman and also performed in the school production
' Twelfth Night at the local assembly rooms. He is credited with writing a school song in
)13 to the tune of the 'Vicar of Bray', which is still sung at OS dinners. He was considered
y his pupils to be a strict disciplinarian but also a man with a very kind nature. Canon Day
illed him a:

*)orn disciplinarian, with whom no boy ventured to take liberties, who had the kindest
' hearts and was at his best in the company of children".*

anon Day also noted that Cowie was:

*nconventional in dress and as unlike a typical schoolmaster as could well be
nagined".*

e was deeply involved in all aspects of school life, serving as Secretary on the School
eneral Committee in 1913 and, alongside Mr Beechey and Mr Pitt, he played in many
: the school cricket matches of the 1913 season.

owie joined up on 13th August 1914. At first, he joined the Hunts Cyclist Battalion but
iter serving on the Yorkshire coast and being keen to be involved in action abroad, he
ined the 7th Lincolnshire Regiment in January 1915.

e was sent to France with the Lincolns and was injured with a gunshot wound to
is shoulder while trying to rescue another member of his platoon, Private Alfred Miles.

e returned to Stamford School to talk about life in the trenches on February 24th
916 while he was on leave. In this lecture, he spoke about life in the trenches, the layout
nd construction of them and the nicknames they were given. He also spoke of how his
attalion was called up from the reserve trenches near Ypres after

he enemy opened up a terrific cannonade which caused enormous casualties".

n the same day as his lecture, he helped with the School Cadet Corps and answered their
uestions about life at the front.

e also regularly wrote letters to the school and remained in contact throughout his
)reign service.

rthur Cowie was killed by a shrapnel bullet near the village of Fricourt on July 8th 1916.
Ie is buried in Dantzig Alley Cemetery in Mametz. This cemetery was started on 1st July
916, the first day of the battle of the Somme.

:eoffrey Jones is buried in the same cemetery.

48

The Curtis Brothers

"England can ill afford to lose many like the Curtis's of Easton."

John Duncan Day. Christmas 1916. Stamfordian.

The sons of Henry Levi Curtis and Mary Matilda Curtis (née Howell), the Curtis brothe
lived for a time in Barrowden. In 1911, the family lived on the Collyweston Road in Stamfor

Henry Levi, born in Collyweston in 1861, was a slater and, along with Horace, Harry ar
Albert, he and his wife had another son, William Cyril, who was born c. 1901 and als
attended the school, and three daughters, Alice Mary (later, Roberts) born c. 1896, Ac
Winifred (later, Tyler), born c. 1899 and Phyllis Enid, born c. 1906.

All of the children were born in Easton.

Henry Levi Curtis died in 1936 and his wife died in January 1955 in Barrowden.

Their remaining son, William, died in 1985 in Leicestershire. He was at Stamford Scho
during the war and his name appears in many of the editions that also contain the obituarie
of his older brothers. He is listed as an editor of the Stamfordian in Autumn 1918. His brothe
Harry is commemorated in this edition.

Albert Howell Curtis

Private – 8th Battalion – Royal Fusiliers (10394)

1892 – 1916

"His death…has laid a grievous burden on the members of
his family to whom we can only extend our…sympathy"

John Duncan Day, Stamfordian 1916.

orn in October 1893, Albert joined the school in September 1906 and left in 1911 when
was in the sixth form. Like his brother Horace, he became a teacher in Easton. He then
ined Sandwich Grammar School.

bert joined up in February 1916 and was sent to France on 10th July 1916.

e was killed in action on August 4th of that year and is buried in Varennes Memorial
emetery on the Somme.

e was wounded at Pozières Ridge during the Battle of Pozières. This was a two week
ng attack to take the village of Pozières as part of the larger Somme campaign. The
attle started on 23rd July and raged until August 7th.

was ultimately successful and the village of Pozières was secured by the allies.

Harry Reginald Curtis

Major – 11th Battalion – Royal Welsh Fusiliers

1887 – 1918

"The army lost a good soldier, the country a model citizen,
and the school one of the very elite of its Old Boys when
Major Curtis fell at the head of his men in 1918"

JNC. Stamfordian. Autumn 1918.

Harry was the eldest of the three Curtis brothers. He was the last of the brothers to b
killed.

Born in Easton in 1887, Harry joined Stamford School as a county scholar in 1899 and le
in 1902 to study further in London. His father had been injured in a serious accident and
as such, Harry became the head of the family and worked hard in order to support them.

He was well respected at the school, as his obituary in the Stamfordian in Autumn 191
reflects:

"His life was a complete endorsement of the crushing dictum ascribed to Napoleon
the word 'impossible' is only to be found in the vocabulary of fools".

Harry was an assistant master at St Saviour's College in Ardingley from 1909 until 1912 where he had hoped to join the church. However, he joined the White Star Line and became an Officer's Schoolmaster on the training ship 'Mersey'. At the outbreak of the war, he was working at Ellesmere College.

In 1914, he joined the 11th Royal Welsh Fusiliers and was promoted to Captain in 1915 and to Major in October 1916.

He had hoped, when leaving the British army, to join the Indian Army before finally fulfilling his wish to take Holy Orders. It is noted in the Stamfordian that Harry felt that his life in the army was:

his penance for not proceeding to Holy Orders when he held a mastership at Ardingley College".

He was killed on 18th September 1918 while leading his men at dawn. The plan was to attack a position known as the Grand Couronne and the 'P' ridge west of Lake Doiran and Curtis was entrusted with the task of taking the area. He was injured in the arm but kept on and was then injured in the leg. He was killed later in the attack by a trench mortar shell. He was buried where he fell in the Doiran Military Cemetery in Greece, one mile west of Doiran town. The attack that he took part in *"ultimately led to the submission of Bulgaria"* according to the Stamfordian report on his death.

*"He owed much to Stamford School but the School owes
more to him whose body lies in a soldiers grave in a little
bit of Macedonia that is forever England"*

JNC, Stamfordian.

Horace Curtis

Lieutenant – 9th Battalion – West Yorkshire Regiment

1890 – 1915

"A very popular officer and an excellent soldier".

Commanding Officer, West Yorkshire Regiment, 1915.

Born in 1890, Horace left Stamford School in 1908 and went to Leeds University. At school he had won a Marshall and Radcliffe Exhibition, and at Leeds he took a prominent part in the athletic and social life of the university. He took a BSc degree before becoming a teacher in Easton in 1911, like his brother Albert. When war broke out, he was working as an Assistant Master at Buxton College.

He obtained a commission in August 1914 and started his training in Grantham before his battalion was sent to the Dardanelles.

He was promoted to Lieutenant in January 1915 and his battalion was sent to Suvla Bay on the Gallipoli front. Horace was wounded in the leg in an attack by the Turkish forces on August 21st 1915. This was the final day of the Battle of Sari Bair, part of the Gallipoli campaign.

The battle had started on August 6th and had been successful in the early days of the campaign but had proved too ambitious in the long term. The Turks subsequently took the territory so Horace's fate was unknown for some time. It was said that the Turkish forces bayoneted any injured soldiers found in the area.

He has no known grave and is commemorated on the Helles Memorial in Turkey.

Francis Madensfield Davis

Captain – 2nd South African Infantry

1880 – 1917

(Mentioned in despatches)

*"He was a marvellous hero and I shall ever have
respect for his kindness and comradeship"*

G.W Acutt. Sergeant, 1st NC, Maxim Section. 1917.

Frank Davis was born on July 21st 1880 and was educated at Stamford School between 1890 and 1896. He also attended Bristol Grammar School.

On leaving school, he emigrated to Johannesburg and joined the Imperial Light Horse at the outbreak of the Boer War. He was injured in the right thigh at Elandslaagte and the Stamfordian reported in the Easter edition of 1900 that he was *"laid up at Ladysmith during the siege"*. He recovered in order to help his regiment in the relief of Kimberley later that year. After peace was declared, he took a job at the Treasury Office but continued to serve for the Natal Carbineers as a Sergeant.

He was commissioned as a Machine Gun Officer in 1914 and served in German controlled West Africa before returning to his home in Pietermaritzberg after eleven months. He volunteered to serve further but the Stamfordian notes in early 1915 that he:

"doubts whether he will be allowed to go as he is a civil servant".

This was unfounded and he was allowed to serve, joining the 2nd South African Infantry in October 1915. He came to England with the infantry before proceeding to Egypt. He survived the vicious fighting at Delville Wood and, as a result, he was promoted to the rank of Captain. It was this action that saw him mentioned in despatches.

Frank was wounded three times, returning to recover in England from October 1916 until March 1917. He was married to a Mrs S Davis of Albert Falls in Natal.

He was killed by a sniper on September 30th 1917 during the Third Battle of Ypres. This battle began on 31st July but heavy rain caused terrible conditions and the attack resumed on 16th August. In September, the allies were trying to gain control of the Menin Road and Polygon Wood, and by October 4th they controlled an important ridge to the east of Ypres.

The Natal Witness wrote a long and complimentary letter about him which was reproduced in the Stamfordian:

"a glowing tribute to the memory of one of the school's bravest sons"

In this letter, a member of the Natal Carbineers wrote that:

"he was the backbone of most of the organisation that engineered and maintained regimental life in peace time…always willing to work like a Trojan".

The letter recalls that Frank would be involved in most of the regimental shooting matches and the annual gymkhana and *"if there was a party wanting to pitch the annual camp, it would be a safe betting that he would be there".*

He was nicknamed 'Davo' by the regiment and was *"a man of iron"* who commanded a great deal of respect.

The letter ends:

"Life is nothing but memories after all and Frank Davis leaves with me a sacred memory, for I knew his faults and failings, and he has made ample reparation. May God rest his soul in peace".

He has no known grave and is commemorated on the Menin Gate.

The Menin Gate, Ypres. Frank Davis' name is inscibed on the memorial

Oswald Carr Fiennes Elliott

2nd Lieutenant – 10th Battalion – Gordon Highlanders

1896 – 1916

*"He has left behind him the memory of one who strove
not merely to live but to live worthily"*

John Duncan Day – Stamfordian Spring 1917.

Every year, the boys in Year 9 visit the World War One battlefields of France and Belgium. On one of the days, the boys will take a coach journey and stop off at a small cemetery in the village of Bécourt, 2km south of Albert. There, they will lay a wreath and remember a boy whose name is posted on the Head Boy boards outside the main school hall and on several of the team lists hanging in the cricket pavilion. He was clearly a well-respected member of the school and the obituary written in the Stamfordian by Canon Day in 1916 proves the very high esteem in which the Headmaster held him.

Oswald Carr Fiennes Elliott was born in 1896 in Witchampton in Dorset. He was the son of the Reverend John Elliott and Sarah Elinor Elliott (née Skene), who were both born in Ireland. In 1911, the family were living in Tallington where Rev. John Elliott was the parish clergyman. They remained there for the duration of the war.

Oswald joined Stamford School at the start of the Easter term in 1906.

In the 1911 census, Oswald's older brother, John Benson Elliott was working as a bank clerk, and his younger brother, Douglas Samuel, born c. 1900, was at school. His younger sister, Kathleen, who was born c. 1898, was boarding at a school in Peterborough. John would later receive Oswald's war medals at his home in Wells, Norfolk.

Oswald Elliott was appointed Head Boy in 1913 and won the Headmaster's Classics prize and the Exeter prize for English Literature in the same year.

As Head Boy, he served on the general committee alongside Mr Beechey, Mr Pitt, Mr Cowie and Mr Wood and also on the school library committee. He played for the first XI football team as a centre half and in 1914 he was awarded 2nd team cricket colours.

After leaving the school, Oswald went to Cambridge University and at the end of his first term, he had joined the infantry corps. A letter from Cambridge, published in the Stamfordian at Christmas 1914, states that:

"Both O. C. F. Elliott and F. J.Cummins have joined the infantry corps. F. J. Cummins seems to be hoping for a commission at Christmas… To balance this, it is unofficially announced that O. C. F. Elliott disports himself in fawn spats".

He was commissioned into the Gordon Highlanders and served with the 10th Battalion.

Oswald sailed to France with his regiment on 9th March 1916.

In early October 1916, he was in charge of a working party who were creating a new trench system through a newly captured village. The area was under fire but Oswald decided that he could instruct his men more effectively from a position above the construction of the trench. He was walking along the edge of the trench when he was hit by a shell and killed instantly on 14th October 1916.

He was 22 years old.

Canon Day considered him to be an outwardly shy boy who appeared nervous but took his duty seriously *"in the performance of which he would never flinch".*

His company commander considered him to be *"very brave"* and noted that *"He fell like the gallant English gentleman he had proved himself to be".*

In writing to his father after his death, his commanding officer said:

"Your son was a great favourite in the battalion; we all appreciated his high loveable, kind and gracious character. He was most enthusiastic, hard working… beloved by his men, and his private life was an example to all".

As Canon Day wrote in the Stamfordian:

"what finer epitaph could one wish yet it was but what we expected of him"

He was buried in the military cemetery in Bécourt with full military honours. A piper played 'The Flowers of the Forest' as his coffin was carried to its final resting place.

Arthur Cecil Evans

Lance Corporal/Private – Lincs. Regiment (2473)

1882 – 1915

"He will always be remembered as one of those who, placing duty before personal ease, gladly abandoned their civilian work and offered themselves for their Country's service"

John Duncan Day – Christmas 1916 – Stamfordian.

Arthur Cecil Evans was the second son of Frank and Adelaide Evans, who lived at 11 Ironmonger Street in Stamford. He was born in Banbury in Oxfordshire, where his father worked as a journalist. He had an elder brother, Francis Valentine (born. c. 1878) who died in 1894, and a younger brother, Harold Llewellyn (born. c. 1886) as well as two sisters, Vera Ethel Adelaide (born. c. 1889) and Gladys Olivia Agnes (born. c. 1892). The family had also resided on Cross Street in Stamford, where his father worked as a newspaper proprietor and a printer.

Arthur joined the school in 1897 and in that year he was awarded one of the Welby Divinity Prizes. During his time at the school, he played for the football first XI and for the school cricket team.

When he left the school, he started work at the Wilts and Dorset Bank in Sherbourne and later worked for the Bank of South Africa in London.

After his work in the bank, he followed in his father's footsteps and became a journalist. Arthur worked for the Bristol Daily Mercury and later for the Daily Chronicle as a sports correspondent. His brother Harold also found work as a journalist before joining the Army Service Corps in 1915.

Arthur joined the 4th Lincolns in 1914. During his service, he was injured four times in action before he was killed while attacking the Hohenzollern Redoubt on 13th October 1915.

He has no known grave and is commemorated on the Loos Memorial.

Aubrey Edmund Glew

Flight Lieutenant – 24th Squadron – Royal Flying Corps

1891 – 1916

"He was one of the best of fellows and as a pilot absolutely fearless."

A fellow officer (RFC), quoted in the Stamfordian, Christmas 1916.

ubrey Glew joined the school in May 1904. He was the eldest of three brothers all of whom vere pupils at the school and all of whom joined in the same year. Aubrey also attended e Aston School in Market Rasen. He was the son of Walter Thomas and Grace Eleanor lew (née Walker) and was born in South Kelsey, Lincolnshire in 1891.

t school, he and his brother Leslie (born c. 1896) were prominent participants in the chool sports of 1906. Aubrey won the junior hurdle race and the junior high jump as well s playing cricket regularly across the season. In 'Characters of the First XI', he is referred o as *"Another smiter, generally good for a few. A much improved field."*

)n leaving the school in 1909, he worked for two years as an engineer before returning ome to Wittering to help on the family farm. His father was a local farmer and, in 911, Aubrey was recorded in the census as working on the family farm and living vith his father, his mother and his younger brother, Leslie, also OS, who later served as Corporal with the Lincs. Yeomanry in Egypt.

Aubrey's other brother, Montague (born c. 1894) received an aviator certificate February 1913 after completing his initial training at Blackburn Flying School and bein examined at Hendon. Montague was considered too short sighted for full military servic He died in Market Harborough in 1969.

When the war broke out, Aubrey was serving with the territorial branch of th Lincolnshire Yeomanry and had served as a despatch rider. On enlisting with the in 1910, he lists his occupation as 'engineer' for Ruston, Proctor and Co in Lincol They manufactured steam engines and tractors.

In March 1915, he obtained a commission to the Royal Flying Corps. He gained his pilot licence within six weeks and was sent to France at the end of July.

John Duncan Day noted in the Stamfordian that his career in the RFC was *"brief b glorious"*. On one occasion, engaged in combat, he shot down three or four German plane and wrote home that:

"I have now avenged Cowie's death".

He was referring to Arthur Cowie, his schoolmaster, who was killed in July 1916.

Aubrey Glew died on September 8th 1916 when the engine of his plane burst and tw cylinders fell through the rigging. He managed to skilfully control the plane until he reache 500 feet and then his machine spun out of control and crashed to the ground. He was kille instantly.

He was buried in the St Pierre Cemetery in the town of Amiens on the Somme.

Charles Shortland Gray

Captain – 4th Battalion – Lincolnshire Regiment

1892 – 1915

*"It was hoped for some time that he might have fallen prisoner
but all such hopes had eventually to be abandoned"*

John Duncan Day – Stamfordian, Christmas 1916.

harles Gray attended Stamford School for six years before moving on to complete his
udies at Oundle. His father was a Stamford School governor and, in 1900, the Mayor of
e town. After leaving school, Charles joined his family iron merchants business – Messrs
has Gray and Co. – which was situated on St Mary's Hill but also had branches in Wisbech
nd Guildford. The archway into the company warehouse is listed and still exists on the
nction between Wharf Road and Albert Road, Stamford.

is younger brother, John (born c. 1898) also attended the school and died of wounds in
918. Their mother, Annie Parnwell (née Strickland), died in 1906.

efore the war, Charles had served in the Stamford Territorials. He was promoted to
ieutenant on August 29th 1914 and Captain on 10th March 1915. He was in command of
 Company of the 4th Lincs Regiment when they attacked the Hohenzollern Redoubt in
)ctober 1915.

'or many days after the attack, it was hoped that he was just 'missing in action'. It was two
/eeks before it was confirmed that he had been killed. He had died leading the charge and
is body had been found at the foremost part of the ground covered by his company. It is
elieved that his body was buried on the battlefield.

Ie left £427 3s to his father and his sister, Agneta, who was born in 1893 and died in 1987.
harles also had another sister, Ena, who was born in 1895. Today, he has no known grave
ut is commemorated on the Loos Memorial.

John Parnwell Gray

Lieutenant – 47th Brigade – Royal Field Artillery

1898 – 1918

"For victory and peace and in honoured memory of lives laid down"

St Mary's Church War Memorial, Stamford.

Charles Gray's brother John was born in Stamford in 1898, the son of Charles Gray and his wife, Annie Parnwell Gray (née Strickland). His father was an iron merchant of 1 St Mary's Hill and a Mayor and JP in the town. John also had two older sisters, Agneta (born c. 1894) and Ena (born c. 1895). His mother died in February 1906.

John was educated at Stamford, joining at Easter 1906, the same year that his older brother left. He was then a pupil at Oundle School from 1911, leaving in 1915. He became a 'gentleman cadet' at the Royal Military Academy at Woolwich and was commissioned into the Royal Field Artillery in January 1918. He served in France from January to May 1918.

John died on 13th September 1918 at the York Military Hospital in Glasgow after sustaining wounds in an accident, and was laid to rest in Stamford Cemetery.

He left £314 6s 4d to his father in his will which was settled in March 1919.

George Henry Whitmore Griffiths

Private – 25th Battalion – Royal Fusiliers (12946)

1866 –1915

"The bravery and dash of these volunteers was beyond all praise"

Colonel – Royal Fusiliers.

George was the eldest son of George Summers, a barrister, and his wife, Emma Lucy (née Cowper). He was born in Birmingham in 1866 and was educated in Whitby before moving to Stamford School. At the age of thirteen, he went to sea as an apprentice in the Merchant Service.

He served in the South African War with the 18th Hussars and was awarded the Queen's Medal with five clasps. Each clasp represented an action or campaign undertaken by the wearer.

George married Alice Riddell in Wiltshire in 1906 and had two sons, George Edwin, who was born in 1907, and John, born in 1913. The family lived in Lavington, Wiltshire and later in Hanwell, Middlesex. In 1911, George listed his occupation as ex-soldier and 'gentleman living on private means'. When war broke out, George tried to join his old regiment but found it was full and enlisted instead in the 25th Fusilier Frontismen.

He was killed while on duty at the Battle of Bukoda in German East Africa on 22nd June 1915. George was buried with full military honours in Bukoda, in what is now the Dar Es Saleem Cemetery in Tanzania. A General in his company noted in a letter to his family that:

The War Office ruled some time ago that no posthumous honours, except the VC, were to be granted…so…many gallant men, including your brother, are ineligible for posthumous DCMs. Should this… rule be revised, I will remember what your gallant brother did for his country".

With special thanks to Nick McCarthy (OS) for the addition of George Griffiths to the roll of honour.

Victor-André Grivel

Corporal – 12e Battalion – de Chasseurs Alpins

1885 – 1914

"Died for France"

Judgement of the court of Grenoble – 19th July, 1917. Inscribed on his grave.

Victor-André Grivel was born in La Folatière, a town near Grenoble, on 9th January 1885. H was the son of Alexander André Grivel, a farmer, and Marie Josephine Eugunée Aglad Buquin. His father died in 1885 and his mother in 1886. As his parents were dead, h was under the guardianship of his maternal uncle, Georges François Gabriel Leon Buqui until he reached the age of 21. Mr Buquin was an agent of the Grenoble Auer Company.

Victor-André joined Stamford School at Lent 1900 and left in the Christmas term of th same year but remained a subscriber to the Stamfordian. He was recruited for militar service in 1905, as all men in France were conscripted once they reached the age of 2(By 1907, Grivel was a Corporal and had already gained a certificate of good conduct.

He fought for France in the war, serving as a Corporal in an infantry unit stationed jus outside Grenoble.

He was wounded in the very early stages of the war and died of his wounds in a hospital i Alsace.

He is buried in Munster Communal Cemetery in the Haut – Rhin region and his name als appears on the commemorative plaque in l'eglise Saint Louis and on the Carré Militaire d Munster (Alsace).

With special thanks to Nick McCarthy (OS) for the addition of Victor-André Grivel to the roll of honour and th research provided above.

Henry Harrison

Lance Corporal – Notts and Derby Regiment
(Sherwood Foresters) (241519)

1877 – 1918

The Soissons Memorial, Aisne, France.

*"In proud and loving memory of the Tansley men who have
made the Supreme Sacrifice"*

Inscription on the war memorial, Holy Trinity Church, Tansley, Derbyshire.
Henry's name appears on this memorial.

enry Harrison was born in 1877 in Bamford, Lincolnshire. He lived at 38 St Mary's Street
Stamford, where his mother, Alice, owned a pork pie shop. He had a sister, also called
lice (born c. 1870).

ust before the war, Henry moved to Tansley, near Matlock in Derbyshire and worked as
poultry breeder. When he first tried to enlist, he was rejected on the basis of his poor
yesight. He eventually enlisted in Matlock on 28th July 1915. At that time, he was living at
Sunnyside', just off Whitelea Lane in Tansley.

e was wounded on 24th May 1916 at Foncquevillers, and was injured again on 1st July
917 at Cité St Pierre while serving as a Private with the 6th (Territorial) Battalion of the
Jotts and Derby Regiment (The Sherwood Foresters).

e was posted to the 1st Battalion on 23rd January 1918 and was reported missing
n action on 27th May the same year. By the time of his death, he was serving as a Lance
orporal. He is commemorated on the Soissons Memorial in Aisne, France.

Frank Healey

Royal Naval Volunteer Division

1900 – 1924

"We have not yet found an outside left forward or a right half back…
Healey (is) erratic"

Charles Beechey writing in the Stamfordian, Christmas 1914.

Frank attended Stamford School from September 1912 until the summer of 1915. He wa
the second son of George Healey, a farmer, and his wife, Annie (née Havercroft) whom h
married in 1896. Together, they would have three sons surviving in 1911 (and a child wh
had died). The family lived in Northorpe in Thurlby, Bourne.

Frank served with the Royal Naval Volunteer Division from 8th April 1918 until he wa
demobilised on 17th January 1919. He was awarded a war gratuity and his records not
that he had a *'very good'* character but only *'satisfactory'* ability!

He served on the training ship, Victory VI, having signed up to serve until the end of th
hostilities. The Victory VI was stationed in Crystal Palace and was known informally as HM
Crystal Palace.

It is noted on his service record that he was traced to a 'medical department' i
November 1923. He died on 29th April 1924 at the South Wales Sanatorium in Talgarth, Ha
of pulmonary tuberculosis and tuberculosis meningitis. The informant of his death wa
his mother, Annie. His regimental history is noted on his death certificate although hi
occupation is listed as Assistant Preventive Officer for HM Customs.

Frank's older brother, George, served with the King's Own Lancaster Regiment. He wa
killed in action on 20th December 1916 aged 20. He is commemorated on the Thiepva
Memorial to the missing of the Somme and on the war memorial in Thurlby.

We must assume that Frank's death was, in some way, related to his war service
However, his inclusion on the Stamford School roll of honour is still something of a myster

It is interesting to note that his name is not included in the Stamfordian when the chapel i
first consecrated in 1930 and must have been added at a later time.

Ernest Hudson

Private – 2nd Battalion – Lincolnshire Regiment (51790)

1899 – 1918

"To the Glory of God and to the memory of (those) officers and men of the forces of Great Britain… … who fell during the Advance to Victory in Artois and Picardy whose names are here recorded but to whom the fortune of war denied the known and honoured burial given to their comrades in death."

Inscription on the Vis de Artois Memorial.

Ernest was born in South Luffenham, the son of Samuel, a coal porter, and his wife, Sarah (née Hippey). He had five older brothers – William (born c. 1886), Charles (born c. 1890), Frederick (born c. 1892), John (born c. 1894) and Samuel (born c. 1896) and a sister, Sarah (born c. 1898). Three of his brothers also served during the war.

He attended Stamford School as a county scholar from September 1910 until July 1913. In 1913, he was awarded two form prizes in French and science. After leaving school, he worked as a clerk for Messrs. Ellis and Everard Limited, builders' merchants who dealt in coal, coke, limestone and salt.

He enlisted in Stamford and left for France in April 1918. He was killed by a sniper on 22nd August 1918, probably during the Battle of Albert. He was only 19 years old.

He has no known grave and is commemorated on the Vis de Artois memorial in France. A memorial service was held for him at St Mary's Church in South Luffenham a few days after news of his death had been received.

The Third Battle of Albert (21st – 23rd August 1918) had the aim of capturing the Arras to Albert railway. It was eventually successful and extended across a 33 mile battle line. By the end of August 23rd, the allies were edging towards Bapaume, which would be the next objective.

Herbert William Jackson

Lieutenant – 12th/13th Battalion – Northumberland Fusiliers

1897 – 1918

"Enshrined in many hearts"

Epitaph on his headstone. Fins New British Cemetery.

Herbert was the only child of Robert William and Margaret Eleanor Jackson. He was born in Newcastle at the end of 1897. In 1911, he was living at St George's Rectory in Stamford with his parents and his uncle, James Frederick Camm, the Rector of St George's. His father was working as a telephone engineer. Herbert was educated at Stamford before the family returned to their home in the north and Herbert went to the Royal Grammar School, Newcastle.

After leaving school, he worked as a draughtsman in the Superintending Office of the General Post Office in Newcastle-upon-Tyne.

Herbert was commissioned from the Officer Training Corps at Durham University and left for France in May 1916.

He was killed in action on January 20th 1918 when he was hit by a shell. He was 20 years old. He is buried in Fins New British Cemetery, Sorel Le Grand, which was begun in July 1917.

At the time of his death, his parents were living at 5, The Poplars, Gosforth, Newcastle.

Geoffrey Anthony St John Jones

Lieutenant – 4th Battalion – Middlesex Regiment

1888 – 1916

"In ever loving memory. Greater love hath no man than this.
Requiescat in pace"

Epitaph on his headstone. Dantzig Alley Cemetery, Mametz.

Geoffrey was born in Stamford in 1888, the son of Alfred Henry and Catherine Mary. His father was a clergyman and, in 1891, the family lived at 62 High Street St Martin's in Stamford. In that year, Alfred became the vicar of St Martin's Church. He died of pneumonia on May 28th 1899 at the St Martin's Vicarage.

Geoffrey attended the school between 1898 and 1899. In 1902, he was living at the Clergy Orphan School in Canterbury. This is now St Edmund's School, Canterbury and Geoffrey is also listed as living here in the 1901 census.

Geoffrey had three siblings, Leslie (born c. 1892), Anthony (born c. 1894) and Phylli (dates unknown). By 1911, he was studying law at Oxford University and is listed on the census of that year with his mother and elder brother, Anthony, living in Winchester.

He became a Barrister of Law (Lincoln's Inn) and returned to serve in the Middlese Regiment from Penang in Malaysia. His brother, Anthony, served for the Canadian forces in the war.

Geoffrey was killed on 4th June 1916. He was 27 years old and was buried in Dantzig Alley Cemetery in Mametz, the same cemetery as Arthur Cowie.

At the time of his death, his mother was living in Whaletown, British Columbia.

Grave of Geoffrey Jones, Dantzig Alley Cemetery, Mametz

Charles Ernest Knight

Lance Corporal – Leicestershire Regiment (2336)

1891 – 1915

"He was a splendid sportsman, distinguishing himself
at school as a cricketer and a rugby three quarter"

Stamfordian. Spring 1916.

Charles had attended Stamford School between 1904 and 1909. He was born in Uppingham, Rutland, and in 1911 he was working there as a schoolteacher. His parents, George and Harriet, lived above and ran the Unicorn Inn in Uppingham. He had a brother, George (born c. 1893) and a sister, Gertrude (born c. 1896).

At school, Charles was a keen and distinguished sportsman and excelled at cricket as well as rugby. After leaving the school, he returned regularly and played for the OS cricket team against the school in July 1915. He also attended the OS meeting on 31st July 1912 and his address at this meeting was 19, Central Avenue in Worksop.

After training as a teacher at Uppingham National School, Charles had worked as an assistant master at a school in Oxfordshire before moving to St John's School in Worksop. He was at home on holiday when war broke out and, as such, he joined the Leicestershire Regiment, enlisting in Luton and leaving for France on 9th February 1915. He was promoted to the rank of Lance Corporal on 6th August.

Charles died on October 16th 1915 due to wounds he received at the Hohenzollern Redoubt. He had been shot in the arm and the limb had been amputated in an attempt to save his life. However, poisoning set in and he died a short time afterwards.

He is buried in Lillers Communal Cemetery in France, the former site of a casualty clearing station.

Herbert Nettleton Leakey

Chaplain 4th Class – Army Chaplain's Dept

1890 – 1917

"Leakey caused some amusement by pushing his feet through the bottom of the sack"

Report on the sack race, 1900. Stamfordian.

Herbert was the son of Charles Montague Leakey, a General Practioner and his wife, Agne Ledbitter. He was born in Blaby, Leicestershire in 1890, and in 1911 was living in Caisto Lincolnshire with his parents. He joined the school at Lent 1900, at the same time as Victor André Grivel.

During his time at the school, he appears to have done well academically, often appearin in notices about academic success. In his first school Sports Day, he took part in the 10 yards, the half mile and the sack race. He continued competing in the half mile race an 100 yards in subsequent Sports Days but seems to have retired from the sack race after tha first eventful race, which is noted above!

He also played for the First XI in cricket and in 1906 it is stated that:

"As a left-hander [he] made a few useful scores as last man. At times a good, long-stop but on rough out-fields rather poor"

After leaving the school, he became a clerical student. His grandfather, Peter Nettleto Leakey, was a rector in Blaby in 1891. Herbert's brother, Percy, was also a clergyman i Greasley in Nottinghamshire.

Herbert returned to the school in 1916 to talk about his work in Uganda as a missionary. He spoke about the appearance of the natives, their diet of baked bananas and their system of government, as well as the climate of the area. He also spoke about how he won a medal during the Ugandan Mutiny:

"in which, he (said), he had once been killed – or taken for dead, which is the next thing to it".

He was promoted to acting Army Chaplain on 12th January 1917 and continued to serve in East Africa with the East African Expeditionary Force. At the outbreak of the war, Tanzania, where Herbert was to serve, was part of German-controlled East Africa. The campaign fought there was long and difficult and the German troops stationed in the area were often highly skilled soldiers.

Chaplains in the army do not carry standard officer ranks but a 4th class Chaplain would roughly equate to the rank of Captain.

He died on 24th July 1917 of natural causes. He was buried in Dar Es Saleem war Cemetery in Tanzania. This cemetery was positioned near to the field hospital in the capital of Tanzania.

At the time of his death, his parents were living at Goldsworthy House, Gunnislake in Cornwall. His name also appears on the war memorial in Caistor, Lincolnshire.

Cyril Humphreys Leary

Private – 3rd London Field Ambulance (512480)
– Royal Army Medical Corps

1896 – 1918

"Called to higher service"

Inscription on his grave. Bourne cemetery.

Cyril was born in Bourne, the son of William Robert Leary and his wife Margaret Ann Leary. His father was also a chorister and organist and the family lived on Abbey Road, Bourne. He had a brother, Arthur, who was born in 1889 and became a professional organist. His father was a hairdresser, tobacconist and perfumer. Cyril was at the school from September 1911 until July 1913. He received his cricket colours in 1913. He was noted as a good cricketer but was sometimes considered to be unreliable!

After leaving the school, he attended St Mark's College in Plymouth and enlisted at the age of 18 in 1913. During the war, St Mark's College became a hospital and Cyril stayed to serve at his college as a 'drug department dispenser'.

Vimy Ridge Memorial. Charles Lowe is remembered
on the walls of this memorial (page 76)

A reminder of the horror. A shell in a field behind Caberet Rouge Cemetery.

Grave of Edward Smalley.
Templeux le Guerard Cemetery (Page 89)

Classics Teacher 2014 pays tribute to Classics Teacher 1914. Dantzig Alley Cemetery, Mametz.

You who would enter here to worship God
Think of your Brothers who before you trod
This hallowed Ground, and did not grudge to give
Their lives in War that you in Peace might live:

Ask for a heart to follow in their way
Of Sacrifice and Duty.—Rest and Pray.

Memorial Chapel, Ypres

At the entrance to the
Memorial Chapel, Ypres

Memorial to the Missing of the Somme. Thiepval

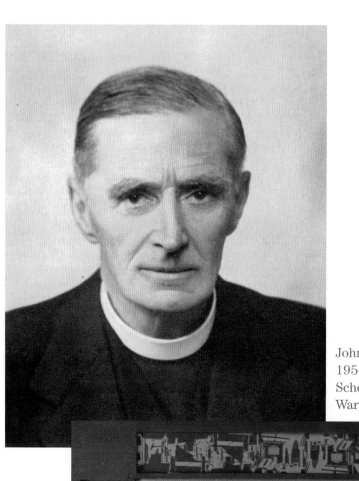

John Duncan "Canon" Day, 1882-1954. Headmaster of Stamford School for 34 years and two World Wars, 1913-1947.

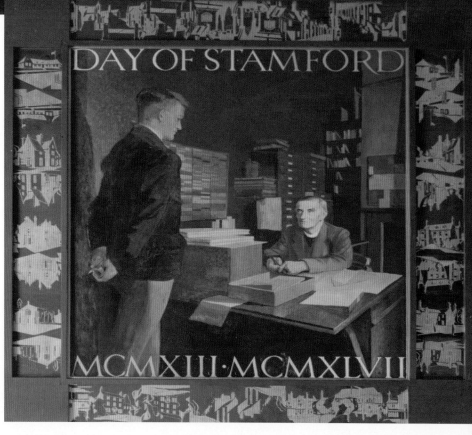

DAY OF STAMFORD

MCMXIII·MCMXLVII

Reconstruction of trenches at Vimy Ridge

Students pay tribute to Oswald Elliott. April 2014
(Page 55)

e died in Brighton on 5th November 1918 of pneumonia and is buried in Bourne emetery. He is also commemorated on the War Memorial in St Peter and St Paul Church, ourne.

e was 23 years old.

he archives at St Mark's College hold letters informing his father of his death. Despite ssurances by the college, his name does not appear on their war memorial and they have pplied recently (November 2013) to try to rectify this.

is medal card notes that a request was made by the Officer in Charge of Records to ispose of his medals in May 1922. This suggests that there was no next of kin listed o receive them.

Dispensary

The photo above <u>may</u> depict Cyril – the man in the white lab coat.
(Archives of St Mark and St John College, Plymouth)

Charles Lowe

Corporal – 87th Battalion
– Canadian Light Infantry (437713)

1877 – 1916

"To the valour of their countrymen in the Great War"

Inscription on the Vimy Monument.

Charles Lowe attended Stamford School from Michaelmas 1887 until 1893. He was born on October 8th 1877 in Ryhall and emigrated to Canada in April 1913.

His father, Charles Conyers Lowe, died in 1887. He had worked as a farmer and married Elizabeth (née Hopkins), his second wife, in 1875. They had three children together. Elizabeth continued to farm after her husband's death and lived at Newstead Farm in Uffington with Charles, her daughter Caroline (born c. 1876) and another son, John (born c. 1880).

Before leaving the country, Charles spent seven years in the 1st Leicester Volunteers. In 1911 he was working as an insurance officer and residing at the White Horse Hotel in Alford.

He joined the Canadian Light Infantry in August 1915 and gave his next of kin as his mother, Elizabeth, who was then living at 14 Albert Crescent in Lincoln. He gave his own occupation as farmer.

Charles was killed in action on September 26th 1916. He is commemorated on the Vimy Memorial. It is possible that he was killed during the Somme campaign which took place from 1st July until 13th November 1916. The Battle of Morval lasted from 25th until 28th September and involved a number of Canadian troops. The Battle of Morval was successful in gaining ground with the assistance of tanks.

William Percival Markwick

Lieutenant – 5th Battalion – Norfolk Regiment

1891 – 1918

"Through death to life everlasting"

Inscription on memorial to Norfolk teachers. County Hall, Norwich.

William Markwick was born in Little Bytham in 1891. He was the son of William Fisher Markwick, a schoolmaster who later became a head teacher, and his wife, Ann (née Jones) who also worked as a teacher. William had six siblings, Wilfred Leslie (born c. 1882) who also attended the school, Annie Beatrice (born c. 1884), Elsie Lena (born c. 1886), Margaret Evelyn (born c. 1889), John Alexander (born c. 1893) and Kenneth Edward (born c. 1905).

While at the school, he played for both the cricket and football teams. In the 1906 season, he seems to have been a regular goal scorer. In that year, he was also awarded a form prize.

By 1911, he was working as a student teacher at St Peter's College in Peterborough. He left the college in 1913. His parents were living at 28 Foundry Road, Stamford at this time. By 1924, his family had moved to 31 St Paul's Street which is located next to Clapton House, which now serves as the IT department of the school. In 1901, this had been the home of the Wright family (see William Richardson Wright).

William married Florrie Brown in Huntingdon in 1915 and was teaching in Norfolk when war broke out and he joined up. He joined the Norfolk Regiment and was killed in action on 4th June 1918. He is buried in the Peronne Cemetery Extension on the Somme.

George Murphy

Lieutenant – Royal Warwickshire Regiment
1st/5th Battalion – Lancashire Fusiliers

1894 –1917

*"Pat Murphy was a brilliant all round athlete, and represented
his division in many branches of sport".*

Stamfordian Spring 1918

George Murphy was the second son of George Murphy senior, who was a Customs collecto:
and his wife, Jeannie. He had an older brother, John (born c. 1888), and three sisters, Mar
(born c. 1889), Jeannie (born c. 1891), Frances (born c. 1893) and a younger brothe:
Charles (born c. 1898). He was born in Kendal, Westmoreland. His father was Irish and hi
mother was Scottish. At the time of his death, his mother lived at Haden House, Haden Hil.
Wolverhampton. His sister, Mary, was a trained school teacher.

eorge (or 'Pat' as he was known) attended Stamford School before transferring
) Wolverhampton Grammar School in 1910 until he left school in 1913. He was
:udying medicine at Birmingham University when the war broke out. As a member of the
)fficer Training Corps, he was gazetted to the Royal Warwicks and then transferred to the
.ancashire Fusiliers.

{e served in the whole of the Egyptian campaign and was then transferred to the Western
'ront.

{e was killed in action on September 6th 1917 when he was shot in the head while
nanning a Lewis gun, after most of his regiment were already out of action. At this time,
.is regiment was involved in the Third Battle of Ypres, a campaign to take the village
f Passchendaele.

{eorge is commemorated on the Tyne Cot memorial. Tyne Cot is 9 km north east of
'pres and the cemeteries around it were used for many casualties from the Passchendaele
attlefields.

{e was noted in the regiment for his athletic skill and represented the regiment in many
ranches of sport.

George Murphy's name on the Tyne Cot Memorial

John Anthony Nowers

Corporal – 26th Battalion – Royal Fusiliers (19415)

1889 –1917

*"As a half is somewhat crude, but with more experience
will do good service."*

Characters of the First XI, Stamfordian 1904.

Born in Little Bowden in 1889, John Anthony Nowers was the son of Ernest Henry Trevo
Nowers, a bank inspector, and his wife, Minnie Elizabeth (née Terry). He had three siblings
William Arthur (born c. 1891), Dorothy (born c. 1893) and Geoffrey (born c. 1895). Geoffre
served with the RASC (Royal Army Service Corps) during the war.

The family lived on the Empingham Road in Stamford and later in Tinwell. In 1911, Joh
was working as a bank clerk for Messrs. Barclay and Co, which will explain his later choic
of regiment.

He joined the school in the summer of 1902. A keen athlete, in 1906, John came second i
the 100 yards open race at Sports Day and was awarded a watch chain. He also played i
cricket matches for the school and was awarded school colours for football in 1904.

In 1903, he was commended in the Stamfordian for his English work after the Cambridg
Local Examinations of that year.

He and his brother, William (also OS) made a contribution to the war memorial tablet in th
chapel that was put up to commemorate the losses in the South African War.

After enlisting on 6th September 1915, John was promoted to the rank of Corporal in th
26th Battalion of the Royal Fusiliers.

he 26th Battalion was raised in July 1915 by the Lord Mayor of London and was mainly for ank clerks and accountants. It was known as the 'Bankers' Battalion'. They were posted) France on 4th May 1916.

he Battalion took part in the Battle of Flers in September 1916 and it is noted in e Ruvigny's Roll of Honour that John:

emained alone with two badly wounded officers and afterwards assisted in urrying them back, for which he received a Gallantry card, and was recommended •r the D.C.M".

e also took part in the operations at Messines and it was here that John was killed on th June 1917, the first day of the Battle of Messines. He was 28 years old. He had been *ounded in the feet and was awaiting help when he was killed by a shell.

e is buried in the Voormezeele Enclosure Number 3, 4 kilometres from the town of Ypres.

is family were living at The Gables in Stamford at the time of his death.

he Battle of Messines was to be seen as one of the great successes of the local campaigns f the war. The target was to take control of Messines Ridge, an area south east of Ypres and ι German hands since 1914. It was also a precursor to the Third Battle of Ypres.

Leonard Ison Pitt

Sergeant – 8th Battalion Rifle Brigade (B/1957)

1888 – 1915

*"He died like a gallant English gentleman, leading
a charge against great odds"*

An Officer, 1915.

Leonard Pitt was born in Poplar, Middlesex in 1888, the son of George and Sara Elizabeth Pitt. He joined the staff of Stamford School in May 1909 to teach Science having studied at London University. By 1914, Pitt was Senior Assistant Master at the school He is said to have been greatly admired by the boys and took a great interest in footbal playing for a local club. He had also served as the school librarian and as the treasure for the sports committee and the general committee. He conducted the school choir a Speech Day in 1913.

He joined up in December 1914 and maintained a close contact with the school through letters and visits while he was on leave. In one letter from the training camp in Aldershot he wrote that he was *"thoroughly enjoying life but found snap shooting difficult."* He also attempted to get his dog adopted as the regimental mascot but was unsuccessful!

He was soon promoted to the rank of Corporal and, by the end of 1915, he was a Sergeant His battalion was one of the first of Kitchener's 'new army 'battalions to head for the front

He was killed at the end of July 1915 while holding some trenches near Hooge. More than half of his battalion were lost on that day.

There was considerable confusion over his death and his subsequent burial. A letter dated 26th September 1915 to the Officer of the West Yorks Regiment states that when Leonard's family were informed that he was 'missing in action' they replied to say that they had received a letter from a Private J Shields of the Machine Gun Section, 1st West Yorks Regiment, who told them that he had come across Pitt's body and buried it. The letter was dated 4/8/15 and written by Private E.G Pusey (for J. Shields, who, according to Pusey had said that he could not compose a suitable letter):

"we came across the body of Sergeant Leonard Ison Pitt lying in the open facing the enemies trenches. I cannot say more than that we buried him where he fell by the side of his fallen comrades. Am returning two photos found in his pockets which were enclosed in a case which for reasons shall not send to you".

He also stated that he had buried Leonard's cheque book with the body –

"I also found his cheque book. Was in a state of decay and in pieces in my hand. I buried it with his body".

The letter was received by George Pitt at his home in Essex on August 18th.

Since that time, his pay book had been received by the OC of the rifle brigade *"without any explanation as to how it was found".*

His grave is now in Birr Cross Roads Cemetery which was within allied lines for much of the war. The cemetery was started in 1917 when the area was used as a dressing station.

He left £9 to his father in his will. His father also received his son's medals in 1920.

Leonard had four siblings – Ethel (born c. 1869) who was also a school teacher, Arthur (born c. 1881), Maud (born c. 1883) and Florence (born c. 1885).

Thomas Francis Senescall

Private – Suffolk Regiment (41221)

1898 – 1917

"Only those who knew the happiness of his home life and his warm affection for his parents can appreciate what the loss of their only son has meant to them."

Stamfordian, Spring 1918.

Thomas attended Stamford School between January 1907 and July 1915. He played in the school cricket team and is noted in 1914 as *"slow but (improving) steadily during the season. Should be useful next year"*.

He also played football for the school and it is stated in the Stamfordian of Spring 1915 that *"Senescall, at outside left, did nothing whatever"* in a match against Lincoln School in the previous October. In a report on a November match against Laxton Grammar, he does not fare much better: *"This match was played in a rain storm and this seemed to take the energy out of the play, Senescall being most to blame in this respect."* Despite this, he did achieve colours for the football second team!

Thomas was born in Bedford to William, a builders' clerk, and Hetty Senescall (née Hill) and he had one sister, Hilda, who was born in 1899. At the time of his death, his parents were living at 2 New Cross Road in the town.

He was considered by Canon Day as a popular pupil and *"gifted with a particularly bright and genial disposition and could always be relied upon to do his best"*. He entered the Kitson Empire Lighting Company when he left the school but was enlisted in January 1917 and trained at Brockton Camp in Staffordshire with the 12th Training Reserve Battalion.

He was sent to France in March 1917 to serve with the signalling staff of the Suffolk Regiment.

He was killed in action on August 27th 1917, aged 19, and was buried in Hargicourt British Cemetery in Aisne, France. The cemetery was started in May 1917 after the area was occupied by allied troops.

Stanley Le Fleming Shepherd
(MC And Bar.)

Major – 6th Battalion – Northamptonshire Regiment
(45th Battalion Royal Fusiliers)

1889 –1919

*"For conspicuous gallantry in action [at Trones Wood on
14th July 1916]. Although severely wounded, he continued to lead
his company with great dash until exhausted. It was greatly due to his
fine example that an important enemy strong point was captured."*

London Gazette – MC citation, 20th October 1916.

Stanley Shepherd was born in Bennington, Lincolnshire in 1889, the son of a doctor – he lived for a time at the Hall in Long Buckby, Northamptonshire.

Stanley was educated in Barkwith, Lincolnshire before joining Stamford School in around 1905. He served with the Northamptonshire Regiment where he was injured six times and awarded the Military Cross and Bar, and the Croix de Guerre with star, as well as being mentioned several times in despatches.

He led a group of men from various regiments at the battle of Cachy Major and the group was known informally as "Shepherd's Force". He was asked to continue his service after the war with the Northern Relief Force in Russia and was killed in action on 10th August 1919.

At that time, he was working in Archangel, a port through which the allies supplied food and munitions to Russia. The allied forces had been sent there to support the Soviet Russian government against a potential threat from the German occupied country of Finland.

Stanley was returning to camp when he was hit by the splinter from a bomb thrown by Russian Bolsheviks from a boat on a nearby river. He was buried with full military honours and is commemorated in Yakovlevskoe Churchyard.

His brother, Hugh, born in about 1890, also served with the Northamptonshire Regiment.

Henry Skelton

2nd Lieutenant – 8th Battalion – Royal Fusiliers

1888 – 1916

"He laid down dear life for the sake of a land more dear"

Epitaph on his headstone, Heilly Station Cemetery.

By 1915, many members of the school staff including Mr Pitt, Mr Cowie and Mr Wood had joined up, and replacement staff were needed to fill the vacant teaching posts. Henry Skelton, also known as Harry, was employed in 1914 and is first mentioned in the Christmas edition of the Stamfordian. During the Christmas holidays of 1915 however, Mr Skelton had also joined up and enlisted as a Private in the Lincs. Regiment. He later transferred into the Essex Regiment.

Harry Skelton was born in Alford, Lincolnshire, the son of Richard Maidens Skelton and his wife, Sarah Ann (née Cole). He had five sisters – Annie (born c. 1876), Alice (born c. 1878), Edith (born c. 1882), Florence (born c. 1886) and Hilda (born c. 1892). He also had a brother, George (born c. 1883) who served with the RGA (Royal Garrison Artillery) during the war.

In 1911, Harry was working as an assistant schoolmaster at a school in Wales and, before that, he had lived with his family in Alford, where his father had worked as a butcher. His mother died in 1900.

When he was killed on 12th October 1916, Harry was serving as a 2nd Lieutenant with the 8th Battlion Royal Fusiliers. His regiment was fighting for control of Le Transloy Ridge (where Arthur Taverner also fell) on the Somme in October 1916.

He was 28 and is buried in Heilly Station Cemetery on the Somme. Heilly Station served as a dressing station from April 1916.

Edward Smalley

Private – 2nd Battalion – Royal Dublin Fusiliers (28203)

1889 –1917

"E. Smalley has not shown much improvement since last year.
He kept wicket in the first part of the season: he has failed to score
heavily off his bat: he should give up poking."

Stamfordian Midsummer, 1904.

The son of farmer Skelton Smalley and his wife, Martha (née Haylock), Edward Smalley was born in Elton in Huntingdonshire in 1889. He had two brothers, Charles (born c. 1887) and Walter (born c.1890), and one sister, Edith (born c. 1887). The family lived in Whittlesey before moving to Pilsgate. Skelton Smalley died in September 1912.

Edward left the school in 1904. He played cricket for the First XI but, as the quote above suggests, with varied success! However, he did receive his cricket colours in 1903. Academically, he won a maths prize in 1903 and in the classics report of 1901 it states that:

"In Form I. Smalley ii showed that he has got a splendid grasp of the elements of the language. He showed greater accuracy than many boys in higher forms".

In 1911, Edward was working on the family farm in Pilsgate with his brother, Charles. After his father's death, his mother had moved to Cedar Tor in Barnack.

During the war, Edward served as a Private in the Royal Dublin Fusiliers. He died on Christmas Eve 1917 in France, aged 28.

He is now buried in the Templeux-le-Guerard British Cemetery in France, which was started in April 1917 after the village was taken by the allies.

Harold Thomas Springthorpe

Lance Corporal – Lincs. Yeomanry (1803)

1886 – 1915

"Fewer old Stamfordians have secured higher honours
in the athletic world than HT Springthorpe".

John Duncan Day, Stamfordian Spring 1916.

Harold Springthorpe lived on Tinwell Road. He was the son of Charles Springthorpe and his wife, Kate, and was at the school from September 1901, leaving in 1902. Harold lived at 1 Rutland Place and had two sisters, Eveline (born c. 1884) and Violet (born c. 1885) and two brothers, Herbert (born c. 1888) and Lionel (born c. 1896). His father worked as a flour miller and farmer.

Harold played football for the school and was noted in 1902 in a report on the match against Sleaford as being in *"rare good form"*. He was awarded a mathematics prize in the same year. He also ran in the half mile event at the school Sports Day, along with the 100 yards where he came 2nd and was awarded with a salt cellar! He also ran in the quarter mile and the one mile open race and was placed 2nd in both of them. Harold also made a number of appearances for the cricket team.

Harold began work at a bank on leaving the school but he was also a well known football player. He played for Stamford Town before joining Northampton Town and playing in the Southern League. He later played for Grimsby Town. He was picked for the England Amateur XI in 1910, playing for England v. Wales. He also took part in a number of tours to Europe with the England team.

He was killed while on his way to Egypt. The ship on which he was travelling, the 'Mercian', was attacked by a submarine and he was killed by a shell splinter. He is commemorated on the Helles Memorial in Turkey.

Charles Cyril Staplee

Lance Corporal – 1st Battalion – Royal Fusiliers

1884 –1917

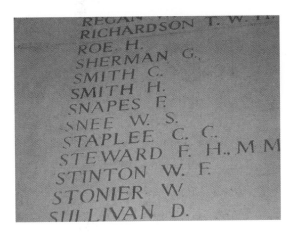

*"To the armies of the British Empire who stood here from 1914
to 1918 and to those of their dead who have no known grave"*

Inscription on the Menin Gate memorial, Ypres.

Charles Staplee was born in 1884 in Barholm, Lincolnshire. He lived in Barholm Manor in Stamford and was the son of Henry, a farmer, and Elizabeth Staplee. He was one of 10 children but, by 1911, only six of the children had survived. Elizabeth continued to work on the farm after her husband's death in 1905.

Before the war, Charles had followed in his parents' footsteps and was working as a farmer. He enlisted in November 1914.

During the war, he achieved the rank of a Lance Corporal in the 1st Battalion of the Royal Fusiliers.

Charles died on the 31st July 1917, at the age of 33. This was the first day of the Battle of Pilckem Ridge, the opening battle in the Third Ypres campaign. It was an attack on German territory to the east of the town of Ypres. By the end of the first day, the ridge had been taken but the German army had successfully started to fight back. The battle ended on 2nd August and the allies had made some successful gains but had not broken through the German occupied area.

Charles' name is now on the Menin Gate Memorial in Ypres, Belgium.

He left £5,078 15s 5d to his mother in his will.

His brother John (born c. 1894), also an old boy of the school, served with the Lincs Yeomanry. His mother died in 1937 in Greatford.

Arthur Fredrick Taverner

2nd Lieutenant – 1st Battalion
– King's Shropshire Light Infantry

1897 –1916

*"The attack was unsuccessful due to hidden machine guns
being left in advance of our barrage line"*

Battalion War Diary 12th October 1916 – entry concerning the day
that Arthur was fatally wounded.

Arthur Frederick Taverner was born in Loughborough, Leicestershire in 1897. He lived in
the Wing Rectory in Oakham and was the son of Reverend Frederick John Winder Taverner
and Frances Emma Taverner (née Turner). The family had previously lived in Upton upon
Severn in Worcestershire.

He joined the school at Easter 1906 at the same time as Oswald Elliott. After leaving
Stamford, he attended Oakham School from 1909 – 1915 where he was a prefect as well
as achieving both cricket and rugby colours. In the 1911 census, he is listed in the school
sanatorium at Oakham as a patient. After leaving the school, he attended the Military
Academy at Sandhurst.

He had one sibling, a brother called Roger Lewin Taverner (born. c. 1899), who also
attended Oakham School.

Arthur gained a commission into the 9th Battalion of the King's Shrophire Light Infantry in
September 1915 and left for France in June 1916. On his 19th birthday, 25th July 1916, he
was transferred into the 1st Battalion where he was to become a 2nd Lieutenant.

He died of his wounds on 11th October, 1916. He had been hit by a machine gun bullet the
day before. The 1st Battlion of the KSLI had been fighting at the Battle of Le Transloy and it

possibly during this battle that Arthur was wounded. He had been in charge of a working party and died in Albert, France.

e Transloy was one of the campaigns that made up the Battle of the Somme. It lasted from st October until 18th October and the aim was to take Transloy Ridge. It was hampered y dreadful weather conditions and was unsuccessful. Harry Skelton also fell during this ampaign.

rthur is buried in Grove Town Cemetery in Meaulte, France. Meaulte served as a asualty clearing station mainly for victims from the Somme battlefields.

Philip James Thrower (MM)

Sapper – 46th Division – Royal Engineers (492082)

1889 – 1918

*"P. J. Thrower, 2nd Lieut., R.E., has been awarded
the Medaille Militaire"*

Stamfordian, Autumn 1916.

The son of a school headmaster, Philip James Thrower was born in Stamford in the
summer of 1889. He had five sisters – Nancy (born c. 1888), Kathleen (born c.1892),
Violet (born c. 1894), Christine (born c. 1897) and Sylvia (born c. 1899). He left the school
in July 1904.

Before the war, Philip worked as a Post Office Clerk. He served with the 4th Battalion Lincs
Regiment before he became a Sapper in the Royal Engineers. Charles Beechey lists him
among the members of the Old Boys Club in Spring 1914.

His change of regiment is mentioned in the Stamfordian at Christmas 1915 but is followed
by the news that he was also in hospital. He was awarded the Medaille Militaire in 1916 by
the French Government for service in the field.

He was killed in action on 17th October 1918 in France aged 28.

He is buried in the Fresnoy-Le-Grand Communal Cemetery Extension in Aisne, France.
The German army had evacuated the small town of Fresnoy-le-Grand on 9th October 1918
and the cemetery was used by Commonwealth forces from that date.

William Harold Wass

Lance Corporal – Household Cavalry and Cavalry
of the Line – Lincolnshire Yeomanry (55173)

1896 –1917

"Greater love hath no man than this."

Inscription on his separate memorial plaque in Tallington Church.

The son of George and Louisa Wass, William was one of five children (including Ida, born c. 1895, Godfrey, born c. 1902, Dora born c. 1891 and Mary born c. 1893) who lived in Tallington. George was a farmer and William was born in Exton at the start of 1896.

After leaving the school, he played cricket for the Mr Sharpe's First XI and for the Old Boys in 1913 before joining up. He enlisted in Stamford and became a Lance Corporal in the Lincolnshire Yeomanry of the Household Cavalry and Cavalry of the Line.

He died of his wounds on 3rd December 1917, at the age of 22, in Palestine (although his memorial plaque in Tallington says he was 21).

William is now buried in the Gaza War Cemetery in Israel.

His name appears on the roll of honour in Tallington along with the name of Oswald Elliott. He also has a separate plaque situated below the main list of the Fallen.

He left £81 15s 9d to his father, George Harrison Wass.

Frederick Whincup

Private – 1st Battalion – Lincolnshire Regiment (18698)

1896 – 1916

"May the knowledge that their loved one gave his life in the cause of all that is best in life in some degree, at least, lighten their sorrow"

Obituary – Stamford Mercury. 1916.

Frederick Whincup (known as Francis) was born in Morcott, Rutland on 30th May 1896 to Thomas Thompson Whincup and his wife, Edith (née Wright). He had two younger brothers, William (born c. 1905) and Tom (born c. 1900). Tom fought on HMS Dublin in the Battle of Jutland in May 1916. His father died in 1906. He had previously worked as a brewer and lived for a time at Geeston House in Ketton, which would also be the home of William Close and his family.

Before joining up in early August 1915, Francis had worked at Martin Cultivator Co., an agricultural engineering firm based in Stamford. He also played for Stamford Rangers FC. He travelled to the front in January 1916.

Francis lived at 20 King's Road, Stamford.

He was killed in action on 4th June 1916, aged 20. He wrote his final letter to his mother on the day before he died. He left £1,555 2s 4d to his mother in his will.

He is buried in Dartmoor Cemetery, Bécordel-Bécourt on the Somme, the site of a dressing station.

Maurice Herbert Wood

(Mentioned in Despatches)

Lieutenant – 59th Squadron – Royal Flying Corps
4th Battalion – Lincolnshire Regiment

1894 –1917

*"Nothing more has been heard of him, and we can
only trust that he has fallen a prisoner"*

Stamfordian, Summer 1917.

Maurice Herbert Wood was born on 25th May 1894 in Stoke Newington, London. He was the son of Arthur William Wood, a clockmaker, and his wife, Julia Mary. He had five brothers – Arthur (born c. 1889), Edgar (born c. 1890), Cyril (born c. 1892), William (born c. 1897) and Eric (born c. 1901). He joined the staff of the school in September 1913.

The Stamfordian of Christmas 1914 notes that Mr Wood had joined the Lincolnshire Territorials as a Lieutenant. He returned to school while on leave and gave a lecture on bombs. He was to earn the nickname 'The Anarchist' *"due to his habit of slipping out at night with bombs to attack the German trenches"*. In a letter to the school in 1915, he explains that he was given a number of jobs because he could speak French.

"they range from going with the transport officer in search of a mule which had got loose, to giving explanations to two gendarmes who found several officers drinking in a café after the closing hour of 8pm".

He also explains that:

"last Friday evening, I was eating fresh pork, apple sauce etc., and reading the Daily Mail, while the windows were being shaken at frequent intervals by the firing of guns".

The Lincolnshire Regiment included a number of old boys and Mr Wood wrote again t the school to describe the experience of being only a short distance from Hill 60 when th attack on this area was being made.

He transferred to the Royal Flying Corps in 1916 and it is noted in the Stamfordian tha he had *"smashed two machines without damage to himself"*. He was mentioned i despatches and this led to a half day holiday for the school on June 22nd 1916.

In the spring of 1917 Maurice Wood went out with his squadron on a photography missio and his plane failed to return. He was killed in action on 13th April 1917 and it is believe that his plane was shot down by Richtofen, the famous Red Baron.

The 13th April was a terrible day for the 59th Squadron – the unit lost five planes an 10 crew members. At this time the squadron was based at La Bellevue aerodrome, close t Arras on the Somme.

Maurice had married Hilda Newman just a few months before his death. His family donate his historical reference books to the school library. He is commemorated on the Arras Flyin Service Memorial.

Maurice Wood left £540 7s 1d to Hilda Wood, his wife.

"The country is very flat and uninteresting, and though we may have
to spend several weeks here, it is by no means the kind of place you would
choose as a holiday resort"

Writing back to the school, 1915.

Arras Flying Services Memorial.
Maurice Wood's name is inscribed on this memorial.

William Richardson Wright

2nd Lieutenant – 1st and 4th Battalion
– Lincolnshire Regiment

1891 – 1916

*"His brother officers and his Regiment can never forget him. He was
possessed of a striking personality and a splendid physique."*

Commanding Officer – Colonel Heathcote.
Noted in *de Ruvuigny's Roll of Honour Part 3*, page 294.

In 1911, William Wright was living at 2 Rock Terrace, Scotgate, Stamford, along with his
mother Minnie Anne Wright (née Barnsdale) and his two younger sisters Emma (born
c. 1894) and Dorothy (born c. 1899). His father, Horace, had died in 1908. William also had
an older sister, Marian (born c. 1882) and an older brother, Horace (born c. 1889) who later
worked in London as a chemist.

In 1916, Minnie lived at 10 St Peter's Hill in the town. The family had previously resided
at 1 St Peter's Street (in 1891) and at 31 St Paul's Street (in 1901). 31 St Paul's Street is
opposite the school chapel and would later be home to the Markwick family (see William
Markwick).

William was born in Stamford in 1891 and joined the school in the summer of 1905. In the school sports of 1906, he was awarded a knife – the second prize in the junior hurdle race. Aubrey Glew came first and received the cup!

When he left the school, he worked as an ironmonger's shop assistant in London before joining the Lincolnshire Regiment in 1911 as a Territorial soldier. After this service he re-joined the regiment at the outbreak of war in August 1914 and progressed through the ranks, becoming a Sergeant by 1915.

He was wounded at Hooge in October 1915 and was promoted to the rank of Lieutenant in early 1916. William was killed by a mine at Mont St Eloi on 21st April of that year. Mont St Eloi is a ridge of land located to the north of the city of Arras. It was a scene of fierce fighting in 1914 and 1915 as the allies advanced on nearby Vimy Ridge and Notre Dame de Lorette. The ruins of an abbey on Mount St Eloi still exist.

William's commanding officer held him in very high regard as, it seems, did the other men of the Lincolnshire Regiment.

Colonel Heathcote, his commanding officer, wrote about him in the Roll of Honour and stated that he had done excellent work in the battalion, both as an N.C.O. and later as an officer. He said that he was a *"splendid fellow who was popular with everyone"*.

He has no known grave and is commemorated on the Arras Memorial. His name also appears on the memorial in St Mary's Church, Stamford.

His mother died in Birmingham in 1942.

Frederick Henry Young
(MC and Bar)

Temporary Captain – 3rd Battalion
– Lincolnshire Regiment (also 1st Battalion)

1898 – 1918

*"This Officer's courage, leadership and initiative were responsible
in no small measure for the successful withdrawal of the (Battalion)."*

Bar to the Military Cross citation, 1918.

Frederick Henry Young was born in the spring of 1898. He was the son of Henry Foster Young, a grocer and his wife, Ada (née Hill). The family lived at 25 Empingham Road in 1911 and continued to reside there throughout the war years. Frederick played cricket a number of times for the school during the 1914 season. He had joined up by the summer of 1915.

Frederick had five younger siblings, Kathleen (born c. 1899), Marjorie (born c. 1899), Alec (born c. 1904), Edward (born c. 1901) and Norah (born c. 1905). He was awarded the Military Cross and Bar on 27th May 1918 while fighting for the 1st Battalion Lincs Regiment at Cormicy.

Under heavy fire, he was able to collect and deliver important information and find a line of withdrawal for himself and 30 of his men. He then attacked the enemy and *"held them at bay"* until the battalion was safe.

He was killed, aged 20, on 25th August 1918. He is buried in Mailly Wood Cemetery on the Somme. The cemetery is located on the outskirts of the village of Mailly – Maillet and is hidden from the main road and sheltered by trees. In 1918, the front line was very close to the cemetery during the German attack on nearby Amiens.

Frederick left £312 6s 3d to his father in his will, which was settled in November 1918.

Grave of Frederick Young. Mailly Wood Cemetery

Bibliography

General References:

www.ancestry.co.uk

www.cwgc.co.uk

www.findmypast.co.uk

The Stamfordian Magazine

The London Gazette

The Stamford Mercury

Canadian Archives – National Archives of Canada

The National Archives

Northampton Chronicle Archives

http://www.roll-of-honour.com/Lincolnshire/StamfordSchool.html

www.canadiangreatwarproject.com

General Record Office (B,M,D Index)

History of Stamford School by B.L Deed (1982)

The Long, Long Trail – World War One Website

Australian War Memorial Online

Tommy by Richard Holmes

1914 – 1918 The History of the First World War by David Stevenson

Archives of New Zealand Online

Museum of Lincolnshire Life, Lincoln.

In Flanders Field Museum, Ypres.

KSLI Regimental Diary

Gordon Highlanders Museum, Aberdeen

The Western Front by Richard Holmes

The Imperial War Museum

Specific References:

http://1914-1918.invisionzone.com/forums/index.php?showtopic=26003 (John Andrews)

http://www.1914-1918.net/bat22.htm (Walter Arnold)

Brothers in War by Michael Walsh (The Beechey Brothers)

Museum of Lincolnshire Life, Lincoln (Beechey Brothers)

http://www.forces-war-records.co.uk/unit-info/475/ (Albert Blades)

http://www.theguardian.com/world/2009/aug/19/battle-of-fromelles-graves-found (Battle of Fromelles - Albert Blades)

http://www.chilliwack.museum.bc.ca/WW1_b_names.html (Charles Branwhite)

http://www.veterans.gc.ca/eng/remembrance/memorials/canadian-virtual-war-memorial/detail/496973 (Charles Branwhite - picture)

http://www.ww1battlefields.co.uk/flanders/passchendaele.html (Charles Evelyn Branwhite)

http://www.theaerodrome.com/aces/england/claydon.php (Arthur Claydon)

http://southamptoncenotaph.com/cyril-shakespeare-clulee/ (Cyril Clulee)

http://www.findagrave.com/cgi-bin/fg.cgi?page=mr&MRid=426307 (Cyril Clulee – grave photo. Permission granted – with thanks.)

http://muse.aucklandmuseum.com/databases/Cenotaph/2788.detail (Cyril Clulee)

http://ndhadeliver.natlib.govt.nz/delivery/DeliveryManagerServlet?dps_pid=IE13344018 (Cyril Clulee)

http://www.blundells.org/archive/in-memoriam/cowie_aws.html http://www.huntscycles.co.uk/Officers/C/A%20W%20S%20Cowie.htm (Arthur Cowie)

https://www.awm.gov.au/units/event_72.asp (Albert Curtis - Battle of Pozières)

http://www.masonicgreatwarproject.org.uk/writeup.php?string=726 (Harry Curtis)

http://www.earlyaviators.com/eglew.htm (Glew)

Tansley Remembered by Keith Taylor (Henry Harrison)

http://tansleychurch.org.uk/warmem.html (Henry Harrison)

http://www.theygavetheirtoday.com/army-chaplains-ww1.html (Herbert Leakey)

http://anglinginthearchives.wordpress.com/2013/11/11/a-hundred-years-old-promise/ (Cyril Leary)

Archives of St Mark and St John College, Plymouth (Cyril Leary)

http://www.yourlocalhistory.co.uk/blog/2011/2/15/lest-we-forget-norfolk-teachers-who-died-in-the-great-war.html (William Markwick)

http://www.activehistory.co.uk/Miscellaneous/wulfsww1/obits/murphy_g.htm (George Murphy)

http://archive.thetablet.co.uk/article/29th-september-1917/20/et-c1etera (George Murphy)

https://sites.google.com/site/unsworthpolewarmemorial/unsworth-war-memorial/Home/1-5th-lancashire-fusiliers-ww1-roll-of-honour (George Murphy)

http://www.wartimememoriesproject.com/greatwar/allied/royalfusiliers26-gw.php (John Nowers)

http://www.cwgc.org/ypres/content.asp?menuid=36&submenuid=38&id=21&menuname=Pilckem%20Ridge&menu=subsub (Charles Staplee)

http://www.theygavetheirtoday.com/oakham-school-wwi.html (Arthur Taverner)

http://www.cwgc.org/somme/content.asp?menuid=30&id=30&menuname=Le+Transloy&menu=main (Arthur Taverner – Battle of Le Transloy)

http://www.shropshireregimentalmuseum.co.uk/regimental-history/shropshire-light-infantry/reasearching-the-ksli-in-the-great-war/ (Arthur Taverner)

http://www.theygavetheirtoday.com/oakham-school-wwi.html (War diary quote – Arthur Taverner)

Inconnu

(After Thièpval)

Loved nurtured and blessed
by creation's cradle;
held tight and adored
lit by a cold bright sun.

Once in a mother's arms,
tenderness lost on the wind.
The known touch
which aches to be once more.

Life that once was
remembered, now by none
but those who see
for a moment. Inconnu.

By Rev. Mark Goodman
(Chaplain of Stamford School)

(For Geoffrey Brown. In grateful thanks.)